Sarah Palin and the Wasilla Warriors

Also by Mike Shropshire

The Last Real Season:
A Hilarious Look Back at 1975—When Major
Leaguers Made Peanuts, the Umpires Wore Red,
and Billy Martin Terrorized Everyone

Runnin' with the Big Dogs:
The True, Unvarnished Story of the Texas-Oklahoma
Football Wars

When the Tuna Went Down to Texas:
How Bill Parcells Led the Cowboys Back to
the Promised Land

The Pro: A Golf Novel

The Ice Bowl:
The Dallas Cowboys and the Green Bay Packers
Season

Seasons in Hell:
With Billy Martin, Whitey Herzog and "The Worst
Baseball Team in History"—The 1973–1975 Texas
Rangers

The Thorny Rose of Texas:
An Intimate Portrait of Governor Ann Richards

SARAH PALIN
and the Wasilla Warriors

The True Story
of the Improbable
1982 Alaska State
Basketball Championship

Mike Shropshire

ST. MARTIN'S PRESS 🦅 NEW YORK

www.stmartins.com

Design by William Ruoto

LIBRARY OF CONGRESS CATALOGING-IN-PUBLICATION DATA

Shropshire, Mike.
    Sarah Palin and the Wasilla Warriors : the true story of the improbable 1982 Alaska State basketball championship / Mike Shropshire.—1st ed.
        p. cm.
    ISBN 978-0-312-60424-0 (hardcover)
    ISBN 978-1-4299-4923-1 (e-book)
    1. Wasilla Warriors (Basketball Team)—History.   2. Wasilla High School (Wasilla, Alaska)—Basketball—History.   3. Basketball— Alaska—Wasilla—History.   4. Basketball—Tournaments—Alaska— History.   5. Palin, Sarah, 1964–   6. Governors—Alaska—Biography. 7. Women governors—Alaska—Biography.   8. Vice-Presidential candidates—United States—Biography.   I. Title.
    GV885.73.W22S47 2012
    973.931092—dc23
    [B]
                                                                2011041103

First Edition: March 2012

10 9 8 7 6 5 4 3 2 1

Author's Note

My oldest son, Michael Shropshire Junior, was born a
week before Christmas 1966.

Shortly after his arrival, he was diagnosed with a significant heart defect. A surgeon named Jackson Cagle performed
an operation on Michael when he was eight days old, a
procedure called a Blalock-Taussig shunt. It left a scar that
ran horizontally from the middle of the baby's back across
to the center of his chest. The purpose of that was not to
cure the condition, but to allow Michael to stay alive until
he was old enough and big enough to survive actual open-
heart surgery.

That happened at the Texas Heart Institute in Houston
when Michael was age five. He barely lived through the
first night, and two weeks later he nearly died again of con-
gestive heart failure. It was later determined that the operation had not accomplished what the doctors had hoped.
The prognosis was that Michael would be left with very

limited physical tolerances, and that his life expectancy probably would not extend beyond early adulthood.

Michael was small and conspicuously frail throughout his life, and he had difficulty even climbing a flight of stairs without becoming nearly exhausted. I worried that any kind of real overexertion might kill him. It frankly used to scare me when my own father, after a few cocktails, would take Michael out into the 100-degree-plus Texas afternoons to play Wiffle ball. The only question in my mind was which of them would pass out first. Michael had created his own one-man team that he called Dairy Queen, and he enjoyed those games so much that I could never bring myself to suggest that they quit.

During his childhood and throughout his life, Michael never complained about his disability. In grade school, he mentioned that he was the only kid he knew who had a heart defect and he thought it was "cool."

The difficulty that he encountered, as do most physically challenged young people, was the inability to establish himself within a real peer group. He grew older and, into his early teenage years, his isolation from the so-called normal kids became more distinct. More than anything, Michael desired friendships with people of his own age, and that wasn't happening. Because of the extent of his handicap, he couldn't drive a car, much less ride a bike. In junior high school, he looked so weak that he was usually sent home at noon.

His peer-group issue became even more complicated in high school. Michael was enrolled in Highland Park in Dallas, where many, although not all, of the students were products of some of the most affluent families in the United States. Highland Park was a place that was known for being, and not particularly admired for, a school populated by overprivileged students of advanced sophistication who spent the Christmas holidays skiing in Switzerland. When the football team competed in a playoff road game in Odessa against Permian High of *Friday Night Lights* renown, the entire student body followed them out there in a caravan— of chartered 727s.

At first, I was completely convinced that Highland Park was the worst possible place for Michael to attend high school, and the principal told me as much. Then Michael got lucky. The basketball coach, Bo Snowden, agreed to put Michael to work as equipment manager for his varsity team. Michael's life improved in a hurry, and during the season, one of the team's best players, Scott Sexton, invited him to join the Highland Park chapter of the Fellowship of Christian Athletes. From there, Michael also became part of a faith-based group called K-Life that paid no attention to his physical shortcomings and welcomed him in. When he got on a bus for a two-week retreat at a church camp in East Texas, I had never seen him so happy and fulfilled. The boy without anyone to play with found himself with more friends, and more invitations to go places and do things, than he could handle. They gave him hope, and they gave him confidence, enough so that he wrote a fan letter to country and western music star Tanya Tucker, initiating an exchange of correspondence between them that went on for years.

After high school, Michael stayed involved with K-Life, and he stayed in close touch with the Christian kids who provided him with true and enduring friendships. Michael's physical condition, as the heart doctors in Houston had predicted, finally began to deteriorate—and rapidly. He spent the better part of 1999 at Presbyterian Hospital in Dallas, and a steady flow of his friends from the Christian group was almost constantly there with him, offering support, good cheer, and laughter.

Michael was born and died on a Sunday. Some of his K-Life companions had by then entered the ministry, and they arranged and preached a service at the Northwest Bible Church in Dallas that was attended by several hundred of his friends. Because of those young people, Michael's life was meaningful and complete.

In 2008, I decided to write a sports book, which was something I had been doing for a living for more than a decade, and of course I needed a topic. My agent mentioned that underdog stories were in vogue at the time, and it was about then that Sarah Palin was dominating headlines. A couple of accounts mentioned that she had played point guard on a high school basketball team that had sprung some big upsets in order to win the Alaska state championship.

After a little research, I learned that Palin and her teammates were strongly motivated by their involvement with the Christian faith. That made me think of Michael, because I had seen the good that kids like the Wasilla Warriors can do. From my perspective, this emerged as a story that had to be told.

The travels and experiences of the Wasilla girls, and their coaches and community, provided an intriguing kind of sports/adventure narrative, not to mention an opportunity for the author to travel to Alaska.

But the real foundation of this book is a tribute to those K-Life kids in Dallas and the others just like them around the country. They will always have my utmost and lasting respect.

Preface

Antlers! Antlers!"

Chuck Heath of Wasilla, Alaska, is giving commands to Bo, his almost one-year-old black Labrador retriever. He is conducting a sort of training exercise, the purpose of the drill being for Bo to locate and fetch some portion of an antler from a moose or an elk or a caribou that might be found in the ample yard of Heath's home. He lives in a cul-de-sac not far from the Palmer-Wasilla Highway. An all-terrain vehicle the size of a small Sherman tank is parked in the garage.

If creative lawn decoration is the art form that many consider it to be, then Chuck Heath's house is the Louvre. Large, imaginatively arranged cone-shaped structures, perhaps ten feet high, composed entirely of antlers, are strategically placed around the property. Similarly shaped displays are constructed of round fishing buoys. This is the ultimate presentation of rustic wildlife sculpture.

Bo prances actively about the premises, unearths a find
that might please his master, and brings it back. The item
in his mouth is not an antler, though. It is a desiccated baseball cap, an artifact that might have been buried beneath
the snows of quite a few Alaskan winters. Chuck Heath
stares at the dog, who is plainly eager to please. Then he
laughs and shakes his head. He is a career teacher and coach,
and he knows that no matter how hard a kid tries, sometimes mistakes will be made. He tethers the dog and goes
inside to check on his wife, Sally. Just a half hour before,
he'd brought Sally home from the Wasilla hospital where
she had undergone a hip replacement.

Sally is up and moving around the house with the aid
of a walker, but it was hardly evident that she'd just come
out of a major orthopedic procedure. The hospital had sent
Sally home with a bottle of pain pills, but she was refusing
to take them. There is another caller in the house checking
on Sally. She is introduced as "Sarah's senator," the Wasilla
area representative to the legislature in Juneau. Quite a few
visitors come through the Heath household, since they are
the parents of Sarah Palin, the former governor of Alaska
who achieved overnight political rock star status in 2008,
when John McCain selected her from frozen obscurity to
become his presidential running mate.

Chuck Heath is not afraid to talk to the media, but he
told me, "I've been burned quite a few times." He is really

not sure whom he can trust anymore, but he invited me to the house after I had found his home number listed in the Wasilla phone directory. I called him and said I was a relatively harmless sixty-eight-year-old sportswriter. "That's not old. Come on over," he said, and gave directions to the house.

The interior of the Heath homestead is as striking as the landscape features. The wall of the den is adorned with a jaw-dropping assembly of trophies, pelts and animal heads, snakeskins, and several species of large fish. It is glaringly evident that Chuck Heath's favorite hobby is not playing the cello.

The man is about as open, friendly, and candid as anybody I have encountered in my career as a journalist, and that spans five decades. He talked about his coaching career and said, "There's not much difference between the girls and boys, except that with the girls you can't pat 'em on the butt."

Like Sarah Palin, Sally is a deeply faithful Christian woman. Chuck's ideals are a little bit different, but he lives the principles and adheres to Jesus' admonition in the Sermon on the Mount, where he says that the road to Heaven is straight and narrow, and damn few people make it.

My stay at the Heath home lasted about four hours, and then they fed me chicken enchiladas that were as good as any you'll find in the better Tex-Mex restaurants found in my part of the world. I drove back to my room at the Alaska Select Inn on Bogard Road, feeling good about Sarah Palin. How can anybody go wrong when they were brought up by a couple as genuine as Chuck and Sally Heath?

Finally, I was beginning to feel good about Alaska, too.

I really had not wanted to come. In the past, I had taken on some fairly daunting job assignments. In 1999, working on an assignment for *Sports Illustrated*, I traveled to Libya to interview one of the sons of Moammar Gadhafi. He was the chairman of the Libyan Olympic committee, a challenging job in that Libya has no athletes. And years before that, I had covered a Saturday night LSU football game at Death Valley in Baton Rouge, which is a lot weirder than the Gadhafi family.

My inhibitions about Alaska stemmed from some earlier events. The first happened in 1951, when I saw the horror classic *The Thing from Another World*, which had an arctic setting. That was James Arness's movie debut. He played a blood-sucking monster from outer space, and his speaking role consisted of "Aarrggg!" The movie terrified me to the extent that I went home, hid under the bed, and didn't come back out for two weeks. The nightmares recurred for years.

Then, when I was in school at the University of Texas in Austin, I attended a live performance by the singer Johnny Horton. His greatest hit was the all-time country classic

"North to Alaska." The show took place at a roadhouse kind of place called the Skyline. Horton was great that night, and he sang the living daylights out of the Alaska song. One hour after the show, Johnny Horton was killed in an auto crash. He was driving to Dallas to meet with the actor Ward Bond, star of the hit television series *Wagon Train*, and the plan had been to discuss the possibility of Horton singing a new theme song for the Western series. At almost the exact moment that Horton was being killed in the wreck, on November 5, 1960, Ward Bond died of a heart attack in a Dallas motel room. But somehow, when the topic of Alaska was mentioned, I always recalled seeing Johnny Horton and his farewell performance.

Finally, in high school, I knew a guy named Bobby Hale. In his junior year, Hale eloped with another friend of mine Kathleen Connally, daughter of John Connally, the future governor of Texas who got shot in the same limo with John Kennedy when he was assassinated. Bobby and Kathleen moved to Tallahassee, where she died of a shotgun blast to the side of the head. The death was ruled a suicide, but there were plenty who doubted that finding.

Years later, Hale would wind in up in Alaska, under the identity of Papa Pilgrim. He had fifteen kids, all named after people and places in the Bible, and he would get convicted for raping one of his daughters. He died a while back in an Alaskan state penitentiary. If you want to make friends with an Alaskan, don't mention the fact that you used to be pals with Papa Pilgrim. In fact, it's best to claim no knowledge of him whatsoever.

So, among *The Thing*, Johnny Horton, and the Hale character, that was one or two omens too many for a devoutly superstitious person such as myself. Look what happened to Will Rogers. He got killed in a plane crash in Alaska.

Also, while preparing the proposal for this book, I had contacted Cheryl Chapman, an ex-Texan who moved to Alaska about five years ago and is currently the garden editor for the *Anchorage Daily News*. One of the things she said was, "This state is trying to kill you. But it's a great place to dispose of a body."

So, upon arriving finally in Anchorage, the lead story on the front page of the paper that employs Cheryl reinforced what she was talking about:

> Friends knew something was wrong when West High physics teacher Don Brabee didn't show up at school Tuesday morning. Within hours, troopers and volunteers recovered his body at one of his favorite hiking spots. Brabee, who was married with a young child, died in an avalanche that was triggered as he sledded down a gully at Bird Ridge after school the day before.

So I added gullies to my pre-trip checklist that included moose and bears as things to avoid in Alaska. At least it seemed safe enough inside the Anchorage public library, researching the events of the 1982 girls state basketball tournament via newspaper archives. The library itself serves as a literal palace of Alaskan history and folklore, and I wished that more time was available to enjoy what they have.

In Wasilla, at first, I was about as welcome as smallpox. That was my own fault, since I had seriously underestimated the number of journalists who had inundated the community after Sarah Palin's speech at the 2008 Republican convention in St. Paul, Minnesota.

Nobody could blame the Wasillans. These are friendly people. Modern media people are not. That particularly applies to White House press corps members, who are notoriously smug, arrogant, and lazy, and compete with themselves to see who can produce the best rewrite of a press release. Plus, they are not much to look at. How the legal profession missed out on these turkeys is a modern-day miracle.

Throughout the entire campaign, reporters of that ilk had infested Wasilla attempting to dig up dirt where there wasn't any, and looking down their ample noses at the locals as if they were animals in a zoo.

The people who live in Wasilla, many of them actual

descendants of those Hall of Famers in the Get Rich or Die Trying League who came up in the gold rush days, are proud and independent. They live by an ethic that says: *"Mi casa es mi casa, y su casa es su casa."* They respect the privacy of themselves and their neighbors, and the media onslaught had tested their patience to maximum extremes.

Eventually, I got lucky, not with just the Heath family, but also several people at Wasilla High School, which when it comes to this project, is the focal point of the narrative. Of particular help were the vice principal, Dan Michael, and current girls basketball coach, Jeannie Truax-Hebert. Jeannie is an Alaskan sports legend, a basketball great from Fairbanks who also starred at the University of Miami. Her teams are always a threat to win the girls state championship, and often, they have.

She thinks that one of the keys to the success of her program is that she does not impose too many off-the-court rules of behavior for her players, and she understands that the more you tell a kid not to do something, the more they will be inclined to do it. "I tell the girls that it's hard for me to put them in the game if they're sitting in jail," she said.

The faces of the students in the hallways of Wasilla High indicate a student body that is bright and motivated. The game ball from the 1982 girls state championship game— the first Alaskan basketball title in the history of the school— is positioned in a place of honor in the trophy case.

Unfortunately, in the high school activity center, the yearbook from 1982, and photos from that year, went missing shortly after Sarah Palin became a national celebrity. Could it be that all of that was ripped off by someone in the White House press corps, who then attempted to peddle the material on eBay?

In the end, though, I would gather enough material, and encounter some truly helpful people who enabled me to confirm that the story of the 1982 Wasilla Warriors is everything I hoped it was when this project was initiated.

What the research effort taught me was that the more an outsider learns about Alaska, the more you don't know. The geography, the topography, the climate, the native cultures, the wildlife, the astounding history—it's all too vast to absorb even a fraction of it during one person's lifetime.

I don't know if I'll ever go back there. But I do know this: I have a profound new respect for the people of the Far Country, and Alaska doesn't scare me anymore.

Sarah Palin and the Wasilla Warriors

Chapter 1

The Sleeping Lady.

That's how generations of Alaskans refer to Mount Susitna, a geological masterpiece that has maintained a one-hundred-thousand-year vigil above the arctic valley that contains the community of Wasilla. Susitna reigns as a central character in native Aleutian mythology. She belonged to a race of giants and lapsed into a slumber of grief when her lover strode off into battle and never returned. An image of the contours of Susitna reflected off the serene waters of Lake Lucille—the eighty-acre centerpiece of the banquet table of topographic joy that is the great Mat-Su Valley region—is a picture postcard from Heaven. Amid grandeur like this, atheism is a tough sell.

Before purchasing a one-way business-class ticket to this celestial sneak preview of a wonderland panorama of the Great Beyond, understand the nonnegotiable terms of the payback. Lake Lucille shimmers, shines, and smiles for perhaps four-and-a-half months. For the remainder of the calendar, it's frozen stiff and hard as marble.

But, oh God. Such unblemished vistas. The Grand Tetons of Wyoming on the southern entry to Yellowstone Park arguably ranks as the paramount mountain scenery found in the Lower 48. The Tetons consist of three solitary peaks. If these are the Three Tenors, then Wasilla lies beneath the whole Mormon Tabernacle choir, a seemingly endless array of majestic twelve-thousand-foot-tall spires, a towering, snow-topped array that make the Swiss Alps look like slum clearance.

Wasilla lies about 45 miles north and east of the city of Anchorage, which contains about half of the population of the 570,000-square-mile expanse of Alaska. By post-World War II American standards, Anchorage, with its population of barely more than a quarter-million residents, hardly qualifies as a metropolis.

The Anchorage-to-Wasilla trip involves a quick journey along the twisting Glenn Highway, bounded on either side of the road by vertical mountain cliffside escarpments that extend straight up into the sky. About halfway, a bridge crosses the Knik River, a vaguely ominous swift-current rhapsody of nature that literally sucks the breath from the first-time traveler.

During the late spring and summertime months, this highway is alive with traffic, a motorcade of vehicles of every type and description, carrying happy travelers eager to experience not the great outdoors, but the greatest outdoors. Gourmands of the earth, wind, and sky pour into the marvelous Mat-Su Valley, known as that because its boundaries are defined by the Matanuska and Susitna Rivers. The Mat-Su Valley consists of a smattering of communities.

Wasilla and Palmer are the most prominent, but also there's a collection of small towns and villages with names that tell the world that this isn't New Jersey. Big Lake. Butte. Chickaloon. Glacier View. Montana Creek. Skwentna. Sutton. Willow. Talkeetna. Trapper Creek. Also, there are some native villages with their cemeteries adorned with spirit houses, miniature wooden structures painted in bright primary colors that protect the gravesites of the departed.

Sun-season invaders are campers mostly, driving everything from elaborate mobile homes that amount to luxury hotels on wheels to beat-up pickup trucks with tents in the backs. They come from not merely all of the Lower 48 states, but from everywhere on the planet. Utah. Japan. Tennessee. Wales. Kansas. South Africa. They come to fish, setting forth on an Aquarian fantasy safari. Mostly the trophies are salmon—the Chinook King, the Sockeye Red, the Coho Silver, and the Humpy Pink, so-called because in the spawning season the males develop a pronounced hump. Also, there is an abundance of halibut and rainbow trout. The season opens in May, when the streams have thawed, and ends in September, and for out-of-state nonresidents, a license that is good for two weeks costs $80.

Hiking is a big attraction as well. In the Mat-Su Valley region, people are drawn to the Crevasse Moraine Trail System or the Lazy Mountain Trail or the Morgan Horse Trail or the Matanuska Mountain or dozens of other routes that might well serve as pedestrian walkways into the Promised Land. Up here, it's so quiet in places that you can detect the sound of the heartbeat of the region that Alaskan license plates identify as the Last Frontier.

This slogan, like most things Alaskan, is a profound understatement. For visiting motorists, the Alaskan locals like to offer the following sage tips: Be prepared to bring a spare battery, seven spare tires, an extra windshield, several gallons of gas, and to be on the cautious side, tow an extra car behind you. They like to add that there is no speed limit on major highways, as speed is controlled by potholes, frost heaves, and wandering moose. They also recommend two rolls of duct tape per person. They're kidding, sort of. The only people that Alaskans laugh at more than the visitors are, in fact, themselves.

Wasilla, once a supply station for the fifty Willow Creek gold mines that were productive until the end of the Depression, serves as a way station for the eager travelers, the gateway to the Denali National Park and Mount McKinley. The park is slightly larger than the state of Vermont and

Denali literally translates from Native American dialect to "the High One," yet another understatement since McKinley reigns as the highest point in all of North America. On clear days, the mountain can be seen from the higher points in Anchorage, more than two hundred miles to the southeast. In terms of base and sheer rise, McKinley in fact exceeds even Mount Everest as the supreme mountain entity on planet Earth. It also serves as the final destination for amateur mountaineers, mostly from the southern and southwestern portions of the Lower 48, who fall to their deaths while attempting to scale the monster at a rate that averages four per annum.

As for the eager adventurer intent on exploring the nature trails in Denali and beyond, Wasillans recommend the following inventory of supplies:

- ★ Map.
- ★ Compass.
- ★ Waterproof hiking boots.
- ★ Fleece or wool hat.
- ★ Knife or multi-tool.
- ★ Watch.
- ★ First aid kit.
- ★ Bug repellant.
- ★ Bear spray.
- ★ LED headlamp.

★ Three fifty-foot lengths of eighty-pound test nylon
   string.

★ Water purification tools (iodine, bleach, or filter).

★ One or two small signal flares.

★ Loud plastic whistle.

★ Unbreakable mirror for signaling.

★ Extra clothing, more socks, and thermal underwear.

★ Toilet paper and small trowel to bury waste.

And those necessities, they add in conclusion, are the basic requirements for a trip to the corner grocery store!

No, Alaska is no place for the pampered, mint-on-the-pillow, Chardonnay-and-strawberry vacationer. It's rugged up here, and for most, the experience of a lifetime. For the foolhardy and the daredevil, it can easily become the final experience of a lifetime. Certain newcomers have proposed that billboards be erected along border points that read: **WELCOME TO ALASKA, WHERE YOUR FIRST MISTAKE MIGHT BE YOUR LAST MISTAKE.** Alaska can be brutal and unforgiving. That is encrypted into the state's natural DNA.

It is historically true that quite a few of the celebrated gold prospectors who poured into the land in the nineteenth century did, in fact, become pig rich. However, the cruelty and hardship that the gold diggers endured to gain their fortunes made many, if not most, ultimately question whether the quest was worth it, as they surveyed their bodies for places where hands and feet and fingers and toes used to be before being chewed off by wolves, or before the frostbite kicked in.

Summertime in the Mat-Su Valley provides a setting for joyful expectations. The sunshine beams upon the landscape 24/7, and plant life explodes into a velvet tapestry of flower-spangled glee. Annually, the summer solstice is cause for celebrations of song and dance throughout the state. But the days pass in a flurry during those precious summer weeks, and inevitably mid-August arrives and the gentle pine-scented breezes begin to carry the first breaths of the ominous chill—the prelude of what is soon to come.

By Labor Day, the visitors are in full retreat in their southbound exodus. They leave with their containers of frozen salmon and their stories and their photos that they will perpetually share with friends, relatives, and drinking companions. Those stories are well received, too. The Eiffel Tower? The Taj Mahal? Big whoop. Nobody cares. People are inclined, however, to admire the photo of the fisherman or, as they are steadfastly known in Alaska, the fisherwoman with a glistening twenty-pound beauty that was plucked from some gushing stream in the Kigluaik Mountains or the Kenai Peninsula or any one of the tens of thousands of unsurpassed fishing holes that compel anglers to travel here at great personal expense in search of the freshwater Holy Grail.

Come October and the evacuation is complete. In Wasilla, the traffic abates. The townspeople are alone again, knowing full well that it is time to confront the surging arrival of the Great White Apocalypse. Now Alaska becomes the flip side of paradise, and Alaska becomes what happens when hell freezes over. Very soon the sting of wind will feel like what Jack London described as the stab of a white-hot knife. With the cold comes the darkness, which for the year-round resident serves as the genuine test of faith.

People who came to Alaska and chose to remain will uniformly claim that their only regret was that "I didn't move here twenty years earlier." But speaking to outsiders, they will concede that the treacheries of the everlasting wintertime darkness serve as a challenge to day-to-day sanity and candidly admit that, "The first couple of years, it bugged the hell out of me."

In the months of the seemingly eternal snowfall along the rim of the Arctic Circle, all of survival and well-being has to be centered on a spirit of community. And from Dutch Harbor on the extreme reaches of the Aleutian Chain all the way up to Barrow—the front doorway of Santa's workshop— and all points in between, the crux of community life is the school. The school is the biggest and most impressive structure in almost every town. There are a few exceptions. Some villages contain some ancient Russian Orthodox churches, whose structures were mandated under the rule of Catherine the Great, back when Alaska was still in the possession of Russia during the czarist rule.

There are not any such structures in Wasilla, though, and the most impressive edifice and the pride of the town is the high school on Bogard Road. It's a horizontal, slate-gray two-story building conspicuously adorned on the right front side by the artistically created likeness of the profile of a stern and noble-faced man with a prominent nose, wearing a feathered headdress. He has the countenance of a person you'd best try to get along with, and he wears a not-so-subtle look that tells the world that you don't mess with him. He is the representation and embodiment of the school and the namesake of the town itself.

He is the Wasilla Warrior. A leader of the Dena'ina Native Americans who existed in the Mat-Su Valley as many as ten thousand years ago, Chief Wasilla appears to be gazing into the past, and perhaps frowning at the Russian fur traders who were attempting to exploit his native territory.

Construction of the high school was completed in the late 1970s. This is a place of learning, of course, but the people who designed the school also realized that competitive athletics was perhaps vital to the overall physical and mental health of the kids who attended the school. The gymnasium is huge, large enough to simultaneously accommodate two basketball games and a volleyball match.

On the second floor, the gym is encircled by a three-hundred-meter-high banked running track where indoor meets are conducted in the cold months. Adjacent to the gym and the track, the building contains an Olympic-sized indoor pool that is available for the use of the entire community. The Wasilla school board authorized significant expense to be put into its athletic facility, and they did it right. What they needed were teams that offered the cheerleaders something to cheer about. Wasilla High School athletes, especially the basketball players, were inured to the status of "participant" but never "champion."

The time is mid-October and the year is 1981. The school is still virtually brand new. This is a time of keen anticipation for the scarlet-clad athletes who will represent the Wasilla Warrior. For the previous two seasons, the girls basketball team had come achingly close to attaining a state championship, only to lose it in the finals, first to Anchorage East and the following year to Kodiak. Maybe the third time will provide the charm. It is now when the cry of "Let the games begin!" takes on true meaning.

In almost of all the forty-nine states that are not Alaska, high school football serves as the mainstay for each and every athletic program. While public education administrators preach the values of academics in their various districts, most of them realize full well that they justify themselves to the taxpayers by the quality of their Friday night productions. The football team and the band—with the accompanying drill teams and the gyrating cheerleaders—are orchestrated into a furious perpetuation of pagan rituals rich in the symbolism of violence and sexuality. That's the pride of the town.

Not so much in Alaska. The elements dictate otherwise. In interscholastic competition, with the exception of Barrow, where the playing field is encircled with armed snipers to ward off polar bears, football has its place, signaling the beginning of yet another school year. Certainly, with a male population uniquely attracted to the seductive murmurs of the great outdoors, this state contains plenty of adolescent males who are well geared for the head-on thunder that happens on the gridiron. When the coach says, "They call football a contact sport, but it's not. Dancing is a contact sport. Football is a collision sport," the kids get the point right away. Still, high school football in the Yukon regions is not a religion, not like it is in Ohio, Pennsylvania, the Deep South, and California, where the multitudes come to worship at the Holy Church of the Pigskin.

Alaskan football is the redheaded stepchild. The fact that somebody named Mark Schlereth is remembered as the greatest player in the history of Alaskan football says a lot. Practice begins in August and the season ends in early

October at the latest. Really, football is regarded as an exercise that allows some of the bigger boys to work off a little excess testosterone, bust a few noggins maybe, and that's about it. The Wasilla Warriors football home games take place on a field bounded on one sideline by modest bleachers that might accommodate a thousand spectators, maximum. The visitors' sideline backs up to a dense forest of towering birch and white spruce trees that maintains an almost primeval quality.

The team's principal rival comes from the neighboring community of Palmer, home of the Palmer High School Moose. The highlight of the area's football season inspired a headline in the local paper that read: **MOOSE TRAMPLE ANCHORAGE CHRISTIAN**. The head coach of the Moose was quoted in print that he swore to God that he didn't run up the score. That was a typical Alaskan football game, in that it didn't amount to much, and talent scouts from Notre Dame and Southern Cal were most assuredly not on hand to witness the proceedings. It is a simple fact that on the rosters of teams on the National Football League, players from the state of Alaska are outnumbered by American Samoans by a margin of at least 20:1.

In truth, the coaches and fans throughout the state find the conclusion of the football season comes as a time of near relief, since this activity serves as an undercard preliminary bout for the competitions that stir up the real passions of the Alaska sports fan. These, of course, are the wintertime events. Ice hockey is big. Nordic skiing is hotly competitive.

But the game they really love, the one that ignites the competitive juices and the adrenalin of virtually the whole town, is basketball. It's a sport that defies the winter darkness, where the overhead lights of the gymnasium provide a cheerful reflection off the well-polished hardwood floors. The small arenas become crammed echo chambers and the eager shouts of the spectators generate a feel-good outlet for the woes and tensions of an eternal winter grind like the pop-off valve on an old steam locomotive. Come to the games and jump and stomp and holler your primal guts out. Most mental health professionals agree that ultimately it is more productive to scream at the ref than it is to scream at your spouse or kids.

Rules of conduct for the fans are posted in most gyms across the state. No use of alcohol inside the gym. No throwing of objects. No kicking or slamming the bleachers. No using profanity. No running on the court. No physical threats aimed at players, coaches, or game officials. No disruptive actions during opposing teams' free throws. These standards of basic basketball etiquette are presented for the adults as much as for the students. They are not strictly enforced at most games, not to the letter of the law anyway, and a fan must resort to extremes to get the heave-ho from the gym.

Alaskan high school basketball maintains a deep and

vital historic background. Since the territorial days, people have been peculiarly addicted to the game. The Aleuts and the Eskimos and the more than four hundred tribal entities that populate the state elevate the nature of the competition and the poetry of motion that occurs when the sport is played correctly.

Alaska's first recorded basketball game took place in 1905, in the southeast corner of the state. Players representing the Wrangell boarding school took on a team of U.S. Marines stationed at an outpost nearby. The Marines won, being seemingly more familiar with the regulations of the sport than the schoolboys. In a written account of the event, the referee, himself a Marine, was described as "the whistle-blower" who appeared to be making up the rules as the contest progressed.

When a rematch was proposed, the Wrangell team insisted upon the use of an impartial whistle-blower who turned out to be a local missionary, and as such, disinclined to accept an under-the-table honorarium to influence the outcome of the game. At its genesis, Alaskan basketball was an exhibition in which controversy outweighed competition, and the sport took wings throughout the state, a celebration of life in the Great Indoors. Girls teams were active, too, with the players clad in bloomers and matching tops.

Basketball rapidly became the only real game in town, and that included poker. In the early days, and those lasted well into the Depression years, many of the so-called arenas were not equipped with running water or electricity. Buildings were heated with wood-burning stoves, some actually located within the boundaries of the court, and enterprising home teams used the stoves as a screen to ward off the defensive tactics of the visitor. Most the early stars of Alaskan hoops were bruisers, men's men, with nicknames like Panther Paw, Corned Beef, Big Shot, and Chop Chop, not to mention "Soup" Campbell.

Fascination with the sport in the North Country expanded to the extent that in 1907, way up in Nome, people were said to take their basketball even more seriously than mining initiatives. The Nome Arctic Brotherhood basketball team was formed with the intent of winning the Lower 48 national championship of a sport that had only been around for sixteen years. The brotherhood's bonding mechanism was based on a shared enthusiasm for the game. Basketball was a game that could be played with the same manly gusto as another emerging American game—football—but was better because the outcome involved smarts over brute force.

Bankrolled with $10,000 donated by the Nome business people, they took off for a coast-to-coast tour of the United States in a private rail car, with players adorned in unique fur-trimmed clothing. Nome's itinerant basketball team did not consist of a group of postpubescent young men playing the game for kicks and Coca-Cola. Most of the group were in their mid-to-upper twenties, two older than thirty. One player temporary left behind the operation of a gold stake that earned him over $75,000, and another had ridden with Teddy Roosevelt at the Battle of San Juan Hill.

Their actual purpose was to promote the Alaska–Yukon Exposition, scheduled for 1909, but they won the hearts of the country with their élan and court skills. Playing against college and club teams, the roving twelve-man gang from Nome played eighty games, and won all but a dozen. One loss was pinned to a sickness blamed on drinking Missouri River water.

After a win at Glasco, Kansas, a reporter for hometown newspaper wrote:

> The Nome boys came here like gentlemen, acted like gentlemen, played ball like professionals, and, when they left, carried with them the good will and wishes of everyone with whom they came in contact.

Interscholastic competition, for both boys and girls, flourished throughout the early part of the century. The first authorized all-Alaska state championships took place in 1929. The finalists were Lathrop High School in Fairbanks, located near the frigid center of the state, and a team from

Petersburg, established deep in the Alexander Archipelago in the most southeastern reaches of the state, on Kupreanof Island, not far from the border of British Columbia. In terms of tradition, that area served as the Bethlehem of Alaskan basketball. Keen battles of one-upmanship took place among teams from Juneau, Douglas, Sitka, Katchikan, Wrangell, Skagway, and Mount Edgecumbe. Competition became so keen and bitter that alumni of rival high schools seldom married. These unions, in fact, were viewed as "mixed marriages" and usually didn't last.

A newspaper in Fairbanks organized the championship, issuing an in-print challenge to the premier team from the Archipelago. This region, then and now, is unconnected to the road system and isolated from any civilization that relies on the invention of the wheel. In order to meet the Fairbanks newspaper challenge and compete in the best of three game finals, the Petersburg Vikings first had to beat Juneau in a grueling three-game set and then board a steamship.

This was a meandering voyage that began on a route that carried the steamer along Frederick Sound, then through Chatham Strait, Icy Strait, past the southern edge of Glacier Bay National Park and then out into the Gulf of Alaska. Proceeding on a mostly westward heading, the ship cruised past the Fairweather mountain range, the Malaspina Glacier, the Bering Glacier, the Bagley Icefield, then Prince

William Sound, the Kenai Fjords and a myriad of other awe-stirring natural landmarks accessible to almost all Americans only through the pages of *National Geographic*.

After a one-way journey of nearly one thousand miles, the vessel arrived at the port of Seward on the Kenai Peninsula, and the Viking team still had a long way to travel. They climbed aboard a train that carried them alongside the Cook Inlet up to Anchorage, and then took another train for the almost four-hundred-mile trek to Fairbanks. Halfway, the train was engulfed in an arctic blizzard and sat trapped on the tracks in a snowstorm for almost thirty-six hours.

Almost two weeks had elapsed before the Petersburg team reached Fairbanks. Tired, cold, and hungry, they went directly to the court and lost the first game of the series. They survived final elimination in the second game with a 1-point lead and beat the Fairbanks team by five in the deciding contest. Back in Petersburg, the Viking players were greeted like conquering heroes. The whole town turned out for a banquet in their honor at the Sons of Norway Hall. And it would take years for the town of Petersburg to pay all the bills from the trip.

Start to finish, this excursion to the first Alaskan state basketball finals took the Petersburg team on a trophy-hunting expedition that had lasted the better part of a month. Because of the extent, not to mention the expense, of that journey, the reenactment of the state championship contest was postponed for a while. In fact, nobody attempted it again until 1947. High school basketball in Alaska had experienced a lull during World War II. That was not so much because of a shortage of players. After Pearl Harbor, the U.S. Navy had requisitioned most of the larger seagoing vessels in Alaska, and the teams no longer had a way to travel to the games.

Still, if any one word can be ascribed to the sport of basketball in Alaska, it is *inaccessible,* and the schedule of competition that awaited the boys and girls teams for Wasilla High School for the 1981–1982 regular season would involve some cross-country expeditions not too unlike the exploratory voyage of Petersburg's inaugural state championship team.

The easiest thing in the world to read is a road map of the state of Alaska. That's because there aren't many roads, and at least a third of those are marked **CLOSED IN WINTER**. Most of the clusters of humanity in this extraordinarily expansive piece of the world can be reached only by ferry boats or aircraft, usually equipped with pontoons or skis, or dogsleds, kayaks, canoes, hot air balloons, hang gliders, and snowmobiles.

While there is no verifiable account of any Last Frontier high school teams actually traveling to a road game via balloon or glider, those other listed methods of transport are commonplace, snowmobiles included. The vast majority of teams officially competing in sanctioned athletic competitions are based in communities that are officially classified as "off the road system." That includes the state capital of Juneau.

The state is rife with villages and settlements that are barricaded and locked away from the outside world by the direst circumstances that nature has to offer. Inhabitants survive during the months of darkness with their caches of food and supplies stored in the ice cellars that have been arduously dug out of the permafrost.

No matter how primitive the township, though, the kids go to school, and they play sports. The lyrics, "far away places with strange-sounding names," from a hit song standard from the days of the so-called Greatest Generation, might well have been composed as a tribute to some of the member schools of the Alaska Scholastic Activities Association.

Arctic Village. False Pass. Eek. Kuinerrarmiut Elitnaurviat. Shaktoolik. Russian Mission. Crow Village Sam. Chief Ivan Blunka. Nightmute. Those schools function within districts such as North Slope, Aleutian East, Lower Yukon, and Bering Strait, where athletic competition, basketball especially, is not merely encouraged, it's mandatory. Should the high school be too small to put as many as five kids on the court, then teams are authorized to use eighth graders. That is how essential these games are regarded to the mental and emotional well-being in this land that is so often saturated with poverty and despair.

People in charge of Alaska's far-flung interscholastic sports operations take a lot of pride in pointing out that the games become a social occasion, and the entire village shows up to watch. And, yes, teams and fans often travel to games in snowmobile caravans.

By these standards, the Wasilla Warriors' operation in 1981–1982 stood out as almost cosmopolitan. The town maintained a hospital, had paved highways leading in and out, a public library (albeit the facility was housed in what amounted to a glorified double-wide trailer), a few restaurants, and the Mug-Shot Saloon, which closed its doors each day at 5 a.m. and reopened three hours later. In those regards, Wasilla had a lot going for it. But the reality was that existence here, with the sunshine and tourists all gone, might as well have been conducted on the dark side of one of the moons of Saturn when compared with the standards of life in "The Outside," that being any Alaskan's term from the distant civilizations that exist anywhere beyond the territorial limits of their frozen realm.

Wasilla was no frills—period. If you were looking for fine dining, you'd be better served attempting to find a gourmet restaurant meal in Flin-Flon, Alberta, or Smackover, Arkansas; although on Valentine's Day or a wedding anniversary a guy might splurge and take his lady for a romantic candlelight dinner at a restaurant down in Anchorage where the specialty of the house was fishhead pizza.

The various retail stores, mostly situated on the Parks Highway on a two-mile stretch that's bisected by the Palmer-Wasilla Highway on one end of the town and Fish Hook Road on the other, would not be easily confused with the boutiques and designer fashion palaces along Rodeo Drive in Beverly Hills. Septic tank service centers were big in Wasilla. You might have discovered a moose cow wearing a tutu before you could locate a physician specializing in cosmetic surgery, but there were plenty of chiropractors. Imported Italian designer high heel shoes were difficult to locate here, but snowmobile parts outlets were numerous, along with gun stores and pawnshops. A taxidermist maintained a conspicuously busy operation, and home heating service providers operated thriving businesses.

When it came to the concept of entertainment and nightlife, Wasilla could offer little more than was available at Red Devil and Lime Village stuck back in the Kuskokwim Mountains. High school basketball would take center stage, and with practice about to begin in the late October chill and the snow already falling, the Wasilla Warriors were no different than the North Pole Patriots or the Ketchikan Kings.

Every team was striving toward something that was more

than a goal. It was a mission, and that was to fight their way—Arctic Circle style—into the event known as March Madness, the Alaskan state basketball championship games in the big tournament in Anchorage.

Chapter 2

I t's that crack of the bat, the old horsehide meeting the barrel of the seasoned ash of the Louisville Slugger, that signals the arrival of spring. The tulips bloom, the birds warble their mating songs, the sun shines bright on the old Kentucky home, and hearts are gay.

The telltale *thumpity-thump-thump* drumbeat of the basketballs bouncing off the gym hardwoods offer a prelude to something less cheerful—that being the onset of antifreeze season. A percussion section clad in gym shorts and rubber-sole shoes were making their grand entry. Throughout our proud land, this happens while the leaves are turning yellow and gold, but in Alaska, people are already up to their navels in the residue of the snowfall from the night before.

Wherever, this is a time for compelling anticipation, and the official opening of hoops practice provides the orchestral overture for the months of perspiration. Backdoor layups, charging fouls, ill-planned thirty-foot jumpers and fearless lunges for 50-50 balls lie ahead. The players come to the workouts with tanks filled to capacity with eagerness. They're ready to roll. For the coaches, it's a different and much deeper proposition and they are prone to tap the brakes on any feelings of undue enthusiasm. Examine the face of the basketball coach closely enough, and it's not too difficult to determine that there is tension in the air.

Basketball coaches are practical people, mostly, and among all the sports, usually the most cerebral. Strategy wins and loses more basketball games than any other athletic team competition. Experience has taught these women and men that no matter how well the team is prepared, nerve endings will fray, and as the season progresses, sleep will become a rarer and rarer commodity.

No matter whether the coach is the courtside commandant of the Boston Celtics or the North Carolina Tar Heels or the Wasilla Warriors girls varsity team, the basketball coach is a member of a fraternal organization of shared anguish. The coach understands all too well that sometime during the upcoming campaign a missed free throw will produce ten thousand agonies, a botched call by a zebra at a critical moment will be more devastatingly painful than a left hook to the kidney delivered by Smokin' Joe Frazier, and the half-court buzz-beater that travels the entire circumference of the rim before spinning out will induce a surge of acid that can reduce the stomach into a worn-out sponge.

When the requirements for Vince Lombardi's paycheck called upon him to coach the basketball team at a Catholic high school in New Jersey in the early 1940s, he found the experience so trying, so exasperating, so soul-deflating, that he gravely considered abandoning the coaching profession entirely in exchange for the relative peace and sanity of insurance sales.

Coach Don Teeguarden of Wasilla was perhaps made of sterner stuff. The torments and tensions presented in the dramatics that played out in packed gyms put his digestive tract on spin cycle at times. And he welcomed the times when he worked as assistant track coach, because during the actual meets, there was nothing the coach had to do other than pat the kids on the back and admire their ribbons, if they won any. Strategy? Other than to encourage his runners to keep on turning left, Teeguarden could not think of much else to say. No time-out calls. No drawn up set plays. No anticipating the possible girl-on-girl matchups. No, coaching track was going to be fun.

This basketball business was getting addictive, though, and it was a habit he did wish to break. He'd worked the game long enough to know that all basketball coaches maintained one common fantasy, a shared dream. That was the vision of the postgame setting after a team has won the big one. "That's when they bring out the stepladder, and one by one, the kids climb the ladder and clip off a piece of the net," he would confirm in later years. "That's the moment that every coach, and I mean each and every one, lives for."

That treasured moment, if it ever did come, drifted in an ethereal light years away in mid-autumn. Teeguarden was not a particularly happy man while he surveyed his squad of girls who opened workouts in the Wasilla High School gym. This was not due to any apprehension borne of the brain-busting ups and downs that the season would provide.

Teeguarden disliked—detested, in fact—the first week of practice for another reason. He realized that the time would shortly be at hand when he would have to cut the squad, which in his estimation was an act akin to cutting some kid's throat. So many had toiled for weeks, laboring and conditioning and honing their limited skills in a full-scale program to improve. They arrived at the gym carrying bright eyes and elevated hopes.

Occasionally, a candidate from the fringe would surprise Teeguarden. Over the summer, a player might have grown three inches taller, or picked up lacking shooting skills and dexterity at a basketball camp, or sometimes, almost overnight, a child might suddenly develop into a young adult. But surprises like that sure as heck did not happen with any frequency.

The expressions on their faces when Teeguarden supplied

the news . . . "I'm really sorry, but we just don't have room for you this year" . . . would tear at his heart. He'd ruined the whole year for some really earnest, decent kid and some of the disappointment might linger in the shadow of their psyche for a lifetime. Teeguarden knew that many coaches placed that task into the hands of an assistant or junior varsity coach, but Teeguarden always handled it himself. His theory was that the JV guy didn't get paid enough for that kind of pain and misery.

A man in his thirties who sported a mustache and still wore his sideburns long in the tradition of the last gasp of the hippie generation that still hung on, ever so slightly, in the early-Eighties, Teeguarden was a self-proclaimed sports junkie. In the previous decade, he'd found a place that would allow him to pursue his baseball dream. That was at Western State University in Gunnison, Colorado.

The city of Gunnison was a garden of recreational delights that was emblematic of all things Coloradoan. The internationally renowned ski resort of Crested Butte lay a few short miles up the road to the north. And to the south, a little further along a switchback highway that cut precariously through the gorgeous Rocky Mountains, was a sort of log cabin town called Lake City that certain aficionados of the trout-seeking kingdom regard as the absolute zenith of the fly-fishing world.

While Western State is hardly regarded as a natural

stepping-stone to Yankee Stadium, the name of Don Tee-guarden will not ever be listed in the school's athletic hall of fame. He was on the baseball roster for three seasons, and would later tell acquaintances, "I was never really exactly sure why they kept me around." He humbly conceded that the only thing that separated him from a high dollar job in the major leagues was an overall lack of ability.

The time finally arrived when Teeguarden, almost reluctantly, received his degree and he was confronted with the unfortunate reality that he would have to decide what to do with the rest of his life. Since he was married by then, the idea of taking a year or two off and heading to the ski slopes to weigh his prospects was not an option. Therefore, Teeguarden did what most young people did, and he began discarding the various options of what he *didn't* want to do.

Investment banking? Nope. Neurosurgery? He was never that charmed by the sight of blood. Robbing banks? Well, the hours were good but according to headlines, the job market was already overpopulated.

Teaching school? Maybe. He never had a problem being around kids, since he was still almost one himself, and working at a school might open a door to what he really might enjoy—coaching. And coaching would put him in close proximity with the facet of life that he enjoyed most of all—sports. He mailed out a resume and applications to various school districts and got two bites. One was an offer from a school in southern California. The other came from a locale that seemed to him, at the time, to be more appealing to his sense of curiosity and adventure.

So Don Teeguarden and his wife, also a teacher, packed up and moved to Guam.

No, Guam was not an island paradise laden with Tahitian treats, pristine beaches, and happy grass-skirted natives who happily roasted their pigs while strumming their ukes as blissed-out surfers rode the gentle bubbling tide for the benefit of an audience of tourists, stretched out in hammocks in flower-strewn verandas, languidly sipping mai tais.

Teeguarden had moved into a setting more akin to Borneo than Maui, a strong U.S. military presence dominating the economy. He hadn't expected anything above and beyond what he found there, and he was largely gratified with the results of his decision to locate in an Asian environment that opened his eyes to a culture certainly unique to anything he'd encountered on the ball fields of Western State or in the bistros of Gunnison. The Teeguarden family resided on Guam in a mode of genuine contentment for nearly five years.

In the great card game of life, though, destiny was always the dealer and, as the end of the school year approached in the mid-seventies, Teeguarden picked up what turned out to be another hot hand. A friend from college, an avid outdoorsman, invited Teeguarden and his wife to accompany him on a visit to Alaska. The trip was largely limited to the central interior, the road-connected part, and Teeguarden was intrigued with what he found. His enchantment was so real that, before returning to Guam, both he and his wife submitted job applications seeking positions in the Mat-Su Valley.

Don Teeguarden came away with no results, but within a year, his wife received an offer to teach grade-school PE in Wasilla. Off they went. Teeguarden's expectations were that once he arrived and established full-time residency in the Mat-Su Valley, a teaching post somewhere in the region would materialize. He was wrong.

So, while Mrs. Teeguarden ministered to the minds of the grade-schoolers, Don put that degree from Western State to work. He found employment in Wasilla's neighboring community of Palmer with a building supplies company. For the most part, he drove a truck and made deliveries. After a year of that, persistence paid off. Teeguarden received a job interview with the principal of Wasilla High. An opening had become available for a teacher to take over a course in basic business studies, and perhaps a little PE. Teeguarden was willing and able.

At the conclusion of the interview process, Teeguarden shook hands with the principal, a cordial-faced man named Ed Frandsen, confident that he had landed a job. Just as he was leaving the first-floor office, the principal delivered the punch line.

"Oh, by the way," the principal said. "Along with your classroom responsibilities . . . how would you feel about also coaching girls basketball?"

Teeguarden was flat flabbergasted. His exposure to the sport of basketball had been limited to watching NCAA tournament games on television, and he really couldn't always know for sure whether a team was running a man-to-man or a zone. It looked like a hard game to coach. On top of that, Teeguarden certainly did not feel he was up to speed on the topic of the workings of the mind of a teenage girl. With his future at stake, he sensed that this administrator of higher secondary learning had suddenly transformed himself into the Godfather, the Don, presenting him with an offer that he couldn't refuse.

If there was a day in his life that Don Teeguarden could recall with crystal clarity, it was the first day as a girls basketball coach and the initial face-to-face meeting with his team. In later years, he would admit, "I didn't know anything." He did not yet know the names of any of the players. All he did know, other than that he probably had a greater background knowledge of classical piano than he did girls basketball, was while girls athletic competition at the time was still a relatively new thing, the greatest girls hoops team in the history of Wasilla High had posted a 3–18 record. The girls were as completely unfamiliar and curious about the new coach as he was about the players. "Before we start, are there any . . . um . . . questions?" Teeguarden offered.

Three hands shot up at once, but each girl had the identical question on her mind.

"If we play basketball, can we still be cheerleaders?"

Ka-bam. Teeguarden felt the answer to this totally unexpected question would provide an immediate outcome to his coaching career. He didn't have a direct answer, so he made one up. "Actually," he said, and the pause that followed seemed like an unendurable eternity, "no."

Then he repeated the "No" and added, "I don't think that would work out."

To his everlasting relief, the girls looked him in the eye and nodded their compliance. At that instant, Teeguarden learned the one primary lesson that would serve him faithfully and well for the remainder of his coaching tenure: Yes, these were high school girls but first and foremost, they regarded themselves as athletes and competitors, and what they wanted most was a coach who respected that notion, and would be completely devoted to the proposition of helping them become the best players they could be.

Teeguarden and his basketball girls forged an immediate partnership, a total meeting of the minds. Working together, as a coach and team unit, the Warriors got their brains beaten out. The girls were inexperienced and under-talented, that was for sure, but more alarming to Teeguarden was the gnawing and obvious realization that while his girls were being completely outplayed, that game in and game out, he was being emphatically out-coached. During time-outs, while the other guy was playing chess, Teeguarden felt like he was playing Chinese checkers.

His first season ended as an unmitigated disaster. Tee-guarden's lone consolation was that if the Wasilla school administration fostered low expectations for the girls bas-ketball program, then he was certainly giving them their money's worth. The second season did not seem any more promising. One chance for an early season victory evapo-rated when, largely because of poor decisions by Coach Teeguarden, the women basketeers of Wasilla lost a game in which they'd held a 7-point lead, with thirteen seconds remaining on the clock. From that episode, he'd learned that calling a time-out at the wrong moment could kill you.

It was after this setback that Teeguarden began to envy the 8 a.m. start-up crowd that guzzled its breakfast at the Mug-Shot Saloon, where the experienced regulars started each day with a healthy concoction known as an Irish Car Bomb, which consisted of a pint of Guinness dark ale that was beefed up with a two-ounce shot of Baileys Irish Cream.

Then, in a strange sort of way, a turning point occurred. An opening in the schedule took place during a Christmas tournament way the heck out on Kodiak Island, usually reachable after a five-hour bus ride through the frozen Alaska darkness, and then a ferry trip across the Strait of Shelikt. He convinced the Wasilla principal, Ed Frandsen, to approve the impromptu journey. Frandsen responded eagerly to the idea. Like so many high school principals, Frandsen had once been a coach, and during the numerous disappointing moments of the early phases of Teeguarden's tenure with the basketball girls, the principal made visits to the coach's office. He would provide encouragement, going so far as to tell Teeguarden that he was entering Wasilla as a site for the following season's regional tournament "because we're going to be in it." Teeguarden noted at the time that the principal had failed to confirm that "we" included him as the coach.

When presented with the query about the Kodiak trip, the principal did not hesitate with a response. He told Teeguarden that he would instruct the Wasilla High School athletics booster club to supply the funding for the trip to Kodiak. Rather than take the scenic route, the girls rode a bus to Anchorage, and took a direct flight to the island.

If nothing else, this venture would offer a mind-broadening travel experience for the girls. Teeguarden, in his gut, knew what awaited the Warriors on the basketball court. The Kodiak Bears were among the best that the entire state had to offer. His premonition was right. The contest was one-sided, start to finish.

At the completion of the blowout, Teeguarden was tempted to apologize to his team for scheduling that yuletide suicide mission. Before he could, one of his players approached the coach and thanked him. "We'll never get better unless we play against the best, and that's what we're doing. Give us time, and we'll compete with the Kodiaks and before long, we'll starting beating them, too." Those were words that Teeguarden desperately needed to hear.

The lamp was lit, and by the end of his second season, a team that struggled with a 2–12 record after the Kodiak massacre finished the campaign at eleven wins, eighteen losses. His players, Teeguarden knew, had always been a group of true believers, and the Kodiak experience had served to cleanse his heart and soul of a sense of inner skepticism.

The girls basketball program at Wasilla was in the process of establishing a present, and according to what Teeguarden had learned, a future. An assembly of promisingly talented players at Wasilla Junior High, working with guidance of a smart and no-baloney coach named Jerry Yates, had been racking up big wins throughout the team's age group in Mat-Su Valley competition. So perhaps this thing was beginning to work after all.

That same year, down in Anchorage, at Robert Service

High School, a coach named Bob Ferguson was seeing similar results. The Service girls, after a bleak run of three seasons that had netted a total of nine wins, had hit the .500 mark, and they were on the rise.

Chapter 3

*No person in the United States shall, on the basis of
sex be excluded from participation in, or denied the
benefits of, or be subjected to discrimination under any
educational program receiving federal aid.*

Thus begins the preamble to one of the most sweeping
and controversial measures of legislation in the history
of American amateur sports, a measure both vilified and
celebrated, the law known as Title IX. The effects generated
by the reforms would alter the face of interscholastic and
intercollegiate athletes to the same extent that the elimination of the reserve clause that opened the gateway to free
agency would forever change the fabric and organization
of professional sports in the United States.

Title IX was created as an appendage to the Civil Rights
Act, the cornerstone of the Lyndon Johnson administration
that was passed into law in 1964. That law was designed to

protect and ensure equal opportunities for all Americans—regardless of race, color, or national origin. As drafted, the Civil Rights Act did not address the topic of gender. Almost a decade later, through the efforts of individuals and groups, most prominently the National Organization of Women, Congress would ban bias against females in the workplace.

The final stroke came on June 23, 1972, when Richard Nixon signed the bill that was formally introduced by U.S. representative Patsy Mink of Hawaii, and with that, playing fields, running tracks, gymnasiums, and the opportunity to play and compete were suddenly made available to little girls and young women throughout the land.

Provisions of Title IX guaranteed that girls would be provided equal footing to their jock male counterparts in these areas:

1. Equipment and supplies.
2. Scheduling games and practice time.
3. Opportunity to receive academic tutoring.
4. Travel and per diem allowances.
5. Opportunity to receive coaching assignments and compensation.
6. Locker room, practice, and competitive facilities.
7. Medical and training facilities.
8. Housing and dining.
9. Publicity.

10. Support services.
11. Recruitment of student athletes.

The outcry of those opposing Title IX was generated mostly from, other than the national brotherhood of misogynists, hard-core sports fans who were convinced that splitting school budgets would soon lead to the downfall of big time football, which was the cash cow and bread and butter of most athletic programs. Their Saturdays would be ruined all because a bunch of silly women—who looked funny when they ran, cried a lot, and threw like girls—wanted to go play field hockey.

Plenty of others were convinced otherwise, and nobody more so than Jerry Yates, a coach at Wasilla Junior High School. Yates championed the cause of giving girls the opportunity to not only play and compete, but to excel and win. As Don Teeguarden had learned during his indoctrination as the girls coach at the high school, Yates was convinced that more than anything, many girls had a genuine desire to be taken seriously as athletes, and all they were asking for was a *chance*.

Aside from teaching science and math, Yates had been boys basketball coach at the junior high, and he despaired at the state of disrepair of the girls team, both at his school and at Wasilla High, situated almost directly across the street. That was in 1975. Both programs, in Yates's estimation, were embarrassments to the community. He knew he could fix that, and turn the situation around at the junior high, and he was confident that the high school team might finally start going places, too, since the new coach there, Don Teeguarden, was committed to winning.

Unlike Teeguarden, though, and most coaches for girl teams for that matter, he didn't land the job as an—"oh, by the way"—invitation from the principal who'd hired them for a teaching position. Yates had approached the principal at the junior high and actually volunteered to coach the girls basketball team, for no additional pay. And the task would involve something of a much larger magnitude than merely coaching—Yates would have to create a program.

Jerry Yates's point of origin could not have been more dissimilar to Alaska. Yates had grown up in the 1950s in Florida. To say that the future basketball coach was the product of rural circumstances would be a massive understatement. Jerry Yates was the son of a frogger. On many occasions, he would accompany his father on airboat trips in the forbidding kingdom of the Everglades, amid the water moccasins and gators, on missions to gig monster bullfrogs that proliferated in the swamp. They fetched good prices because of their legs, and Everglades frog legs were the best anywhere, the envy of even the French.

He was also rapidly developing a passion for ball sports, baseball in particular. In that regard, Yates's springtime was located in the closest thing to heaven. His family lived not far from Vero Beach, which from late February to April Fools' Day, was the spring training headquarters of the Brooklyn Dodgers. The facility known as Dodgertown had been a U.S. Navy base, and at the end of World War II, the famed general manager Branch Rickey convinced the Brooklyn owner, Walter O'Malley, to acquire the facility. It was not only ideal as a training locale for the big league team, but they could also use the barracks to house the almost twenty teams that comprised the Dodgers' renowned minor league system. That would enable Rickey, the meticulous micromanager, to keep close tabs on the progress of each and every player under contract, from AAA Montreal in the International League all the way down to Clovis in the Class A West Texas–New Mexico League.

The Dodgers themselves played exhibition games in the breathtaking setup, a natural amphitheater in which fans sat in lawn chairs situated on a green terrace, or just beyond the outfield, the perimeter of which was lined with tall and elegant palm trees. There was no fence. It was a setting that maximized the grace and flow, the sheer aesthetic, which was so compelling to the ranks of the people who were so deeply mesmerized by the spectacle of the game.

To the delight of Jerry Yates, the appeal of Dodgertown was not so much the playing field but the players who were performing on it. As an ardent fan, he was on speaking terms with the likes of Jackie Robinson, Duke Snider, Gil Hodges, Pee Wee Reese, Roy Campanella, Carl Erskine, and the rest of the entire cast of the immortal Boys of Summer.

He wanted to be just like them, and advanced his playing skills to the extent that at the end of his high school career, he obtained a minor league tryout. A twisted knee ended that dream, and as Yates would reflect fifty years later, what seemed like the worst of breaks at the time turned out to be the best thing that could have happened to him. He went to college, obtained a teaching certificate, all the while reveling in a sporting career not in pro baseball, but in the Fish and Goose League. Yates married a woman who shared his enthusiasm for the outdoor life. She was handy with a rod and reel, a rifle, and a shotgun. So it was easy for Yates to convince her to not only travel, but actually move, to Alaska for one year, where they would teach and fish and hunt—"just to get it out of our system."

That one year would become a long one, one that would extend for the rest of their lives. They were happy at first, living in "the bush" in a remote part of the Kenai Peninsula, and happier yet in the more civilized but still rural life in Wasilla.

It was there that Yates would put the finishing touches on a life well lived by breathing life into the sport of girls basketball in the Mat-Su Valley. At first, he attempted to

recruit players from the Wasilla Junior High female elite—
the cheerleaders. On game days, the cheerleading team wore
their uniforms to school. They stood out. From a popularity
standpoint, the cheerleaders were at the very top of the food
chain. Yates decided to make it his mission in life to change
that, at least to the point that the girls on the basketball
team could walk the hallways of the school with the same
air of self-esteem that the cheerleading girls would always
exude.

He had some success. His teams gradually became competitive and after three years, his project had grown to the
point where he could actually put a junior high JV team on
the court in addition to his A-team girls. Yates was in the
process of developing what amounted to a No Basketball
Child Left Behind program at the junior high.

His practices were intense, highly organized sessions
that lasted two hours each day after school, and half of those
workouts, at least, were devoted to the basics of defense. If
ever a person achieved a teaching specialty, it was Jerry
Yates, who had become the Socrates of the Zone Press.

The girls worked the press to the extent that the tactic
became their trademark, and according to Yates, "sealed
them as a unit." Practices were paying off at game time and
after three seasons it became an event when the Wasilla
Junior High girls lost a game. The zone press had become
so overwhelmingly effective that he would shut it down at

halftime, and call off the dogs, in order to keep from running up scores.

Meanwhile, Don Teeguarden would frequently visit the junior high to watch the practice sessions. Yates knew that the high school varsity coach liked what he was seeing. It reminded him of Branch Rickey, back at Dodgertown, appraising the minor league talent and eagerly identifying the ones who might soon be in uniform up at Ebbets Field in Brooklyn.

By the 1979–1980 season, Teeguarden was watching some prospects who truly piqued his interest. One was a good all-around athlete, with good size and a full portfolio of basketball skills named Jackie Conn. Another was a tall girl, Heyde Kohring, a work in progress who should develop into a good, if not excellent, high school post player. Another, and this was the girl who Yates assured Teeguarden was *really special,* was a guard named Sarah Heath. Sarah's sister, Heather, one year older, had been a star and was already in the varsity pipeline to become a starter at the high school. Sarah was just as good. She was the daughter of a grade schoolteacher in Wasilla who also coached the high school cross-country team.

Yates had gone on hunting expeditions with Chuck and his wife, Sally, and sometimes the girls would accompany them. While Yates had long been convinced that the people who inhabited Alaska were unexcelled anywhere in the nation when it came to basic character and goodness, he had never been around a family as substantial as the Heaths. Sally maintained a firmly etched religious identity. Chuck did not, necessarily, but he was deeply supportive of her convictions.

Sarah's forte on the basketball court was defense, and she performed her task on the zone press with flair and gusto. After the whistle blew, there was no downtime for Sarah. This girl was part bearcat. As hard as she played, Sarah never seemed to lose her focus. The coach had never seen anyone like her. She required little or no coaching, because Yates sensed that it was almost as if she were coaching herself. And as such, Sarah was a tough coach, and she became angry on the unusual occasions when she would make a mistake.

More than the court contribution, Yates was impressed with Sarah's role as a teammate. Without really trying, she seemed to make everyone around her feel good. Though he felt that Heath was not particularly outgoing, and certainly never made any effort to try to make herself popular, that came to her naturally. Her likability quotient was as high as anybody's in the school, with the kids and the teachers, too. Everybody wanted to be Sarah's friend. Yates realized that the junior high school years stood out as a crisis point in the lives of the girls, when social pressures often became magnified to an extent far greater than anything they had felt previously, or ever would again. Well, Heath had certainly aced that test, with a natural born element of honest poise enforced by an unusually mature sense of actually knowing who she really *was*.

He'd watched with interest at how Heath had befriended the tall girl, Heyde. As a seventh grader, Heyde was already approaching six feet, and was gangly, uncoordinated, and shy. Yates suspected that Heyde wanted to quit and would not have been surprised if she had. That would have been a shame, too, because as a talent analyst, Jerry Yates was certain that when (or if) Heyde finally quit growing, she would naturally evolve into a heck of a player. But Sarah had always been at Heyde's side, and offered aid, comfort, and "just hang in there—you're going to be great" encouragement.

With this ensemble, Yates's most pressing problem had been putting together a full schedule for the season. The seven junior high programs in Anchorage did not play against outside competition. Around the Mat-Su Valley, not many communities offered junior high girls programs, and the ones that did were becoming gun-shy about playing against Wasilla. So if Yates's team was going to experience a complete season, it would have to travel. And travel required funding that the district did not offer.

His team would have to somehow raise the money on their own, and Yates was averse to going into the commu-

nity to seek donations. So he turned his girls into a magazine sales force, and they became almost as adept at that
skill as they were at basketball. They went door-to-door,
ringing bells and hawking subscriptions to *Reader's Digest*.
At one point, someone suggested to Yates that the people
of Wasilla were developing the best vocabularies in all
of Alaska, thanks to the "Increase Your Word Power" feature that appeared in every issue of the magazine. The girls
worked their fund-raising efforts the same way they plied
that zone press, and because of them, it seemed that every
household in Wasilla was receiving a *Reader's Digest*.

By the time they finished, they'd earned $14,000 for
the program. Yates did not stop there. He and the boys basketball coach, Duke Fowler, organized what they hoped
would be the largest rummage sale in the history of the state.
They encouraged the school kids to gather anything of
value their families no longer wanted. Clothes. Books. Sporting equipment. Furniture. Appliances. Kids were bringing
merchandise with them on the school buses, and soon, the
floor of the gymnasium at the junior high school looked
like a Walmart selling used goods.

Jerry Yates, girls basketball coach, had been transformed,
for a couple of weeks at least, into Jerry Yates, retail magnate.
When it was over, Yates's team had assembled a war chest
ample to arrange what might have qualified as the junior
high girls basketball trip of a lifetime.

It was a six-day, midseason adventure. First the team would travel by bus all the way to Valdez, the final destination of the then recently completed and famous Trans-Alaska Pipeline, the eight-hundred-mile marvel of a forty-eight-inch diameter pipe that was an engineering feat that, if not equivalent in magnitude to the Great Wall of China, certainly ranked up there with the construction of the Panama Canal. After a huge oil discovery at Prudhoe Bay at the very top of the state off the frozen expanse of the Beaufort Sea—the mother lode—the issue of how to transport the product became the technology challenge of the decade.

Boeing had suggested building special, twelve engine airborne tankers. General Dynamics had proposed designing oil-hauling submarines that would travel beneath the ice cap. Humble Oil fitted a freighter, the SS *Manhattan,* with ice-breaking gear, and when that was field tested, the ship was swamped with salt water and almost sank. The pipeline, built across the Alaskan permafrost and rough terrain, summoned an effort of manpower and ingenuity that was tantamount to landing a man on the moon. Because of the completion of the pipeline, Valdez and accompanying communities all the way to Anchorage were taking on a boomtown persona not seen in Alaska since the gold rush.

The journey to Valdez alone was worth a lifetime of memories, especially since it took place during a cold snap that was extreme even by Alaskan standards. It was 50 below, and a big space heater was installed in the front of the bus to enable the girls to withstand what was happening outside.

After two nights of sleeping on the gym floor at Valdez, the girls boarded the Alaska ferry for a voyage that took them across Prince William Sound to Cordova, where they played two more games. After that, the globe-trotting Wasilla girls took a plane ride to Anchorage and a bus trip back to Wasilla. They returned from the trip well traveled, road tested, and unbeaten.

The assembly of girls that Jerry Yates would be passing along to Don Teeguarden was not only fully schooled on the basics of the high school game, they had been exposed to the demands of travel that few kids outside of Alaska would ever experience. They were battle tested.

More important, the three girls—Heath, Kohring, and Conn—had formed something that extended beyond a standard-issue teammate friendship relationship. Theirs was a deeper emotional bond. As they left junior high for the big school across the street, they were geared to do something special. Yates was certain they would accomplish that as well. For two years, he'd overheard them talking about it: "The Wasilla High School girls basketball team is a doormat—but that is going to change when we get there."

Yates, the old baseball fan, was familiar with Dizzy Dean's old refrain that went: "It ain't braggin' if it's true." And in this case, Yates was totally convinced that these girls weren't braggin'.

Chapter 4

By the fall of 1981, the town of Wasilla was experiencing a population growth surge that challenged the identity of "town." The Mat-Su Valley was experiencing growth, change, and transition. This brought concomitant circumstances that were not entirely positive. The Wasilla that had been a semi-agrarian rural hamlet was taking on a different kind of demeanor. Economic expansion and an enlarging population often arrived with a decline in the lifestyle for the home folk, who were so ingrained in their countrified down-home values.

Employment opportunities triggered by the twentieth-century Alaskan gold that was colored black served as one lure for the potential ex-pats from the Lower 48. At the same time, the concept of Alaska was becoming more and more appealing to an ever-enlarging inventory of Americans seeking escape—escape from big government, big debt collectors, big outstanding arrest warrants, big estranged spouses, and additionally endless supplies of big things that translated into a big pain in the you-know-what.

From the aspect of persons seeking to abandon their past, Alaska offered a sensible alternative. Greta Garbo, a long-ago matinee cinema goddess with elevated cheekbones and tired, watery eyes, famously asserted that, "I *vont* to be left alone." Somebody should have told Ms. Garbo that if that was her sincere intent, she should have moved to Alaska, a live-and-let-live oasis of personal independence, where the natives remained supremely unconcerned over the plot details of their fellow citizens' personal soap operas. A radio disc jockey in Wasilla was heard to sum the scene up this way: "This message just in from the Alaska Dental Association. If you want to keep your teeth in good shape, brush twice a day and mind your own business."

There is no such thing as an "average Alaskan." That creature does not exist. There might be a few general characteristics, one of them being that most Alaskans regard themselves as "people persons," just as long as they don't have to associate with too many people. Wasillans were beginning to sense that their territory, their space, was gradually becoming more occupied with humanity. A little more traffic up and down the Parks Highway. Lines that were sometimes as long as three people waited at the cash register at the Safeway. Even worse, thirsty men, heading home from work, often found themselves standing for five minutes or more holding two cases of beer at the Oaken Keg, while the guy in front of him related his life story to the clerk. That was another general characteristic of Alaskans. They didn't like standing in line.

Wasilla was beginning a slow transformation, turning from a small town into more of an Anchorage suburb. Housing in Wasilla was considerably more affordable than in the big city, and improvements in the highway had made the forty-five-mile daily commute more attractive to job holders in the state's only real metropolis. The town made ideal living for many of the civilians who were employed at Fort Richardson and Elmendorf Air Force Base.

Don Teeguarden was noticing the effects of the population upswing at the high school, and this was not all for the good. Not from his standpoint, because hardly any of the new enrollees seemed inclined to play sports. He joked to his wife that if some of the new and unfamiliar faces happened to be some girls who stood six foot six and could dunk the basketball with either hand, he might feel differently. But such was not the case.

Teachers and staff at Wasilla High realized that some problems were developing within the student body. Absenteeism. Drink, of course. The Wasilla High cocktail of choice circa 1982 was Crown Royal, consumed directly out of the bottle. Drugs. In particular marijuana, which was grown in great abundance throughout the Mat-Su Valley during the weeks of round-the-clock sunshine. The small-town feel of the student body was becoming more urbanized. That meant a decline in the innocence factor. The Wasilla faculty could only console itself in the fact that the negative factors were the same as any high school in the United States, and any place that denied it either was not facing the facts or was not telling the truth.

If anybody at Wasilla High had been fostering illusions that the school was a pristine sanctuary of academia and excellence, those were dispelled in the spring of 1981 when two students set off a bomb in the activity center. The explosive device was filled with BBs that stung some kids, although no one was seriously hurt. Anybody in the room when the thing went off regarded that as no small miracle.

At the advent of the 1981–1982 season, Teeguarden regarded himself fortunate in that the girls who would constitute the core of his lineup, without exception, fell into the "good kid" category. His girls were products of solid, stable, and caring families. More than injury to key players, coaches in Alaska worried about family disruptions in the lives of their kids. It had happened more than once on various teams at Wasilla during Teeguarden's tenure, when the parent of a star athlete, with no prior warning, had packed up and left town—left the state even—gone for good, leaving the children virtually lost at sea.

The homelife situations of this group's players were

genuine sources of comfort to the coach. These girls were honor students as well as devoted athletes who played sports for the primary reason of providing an element of balance to their life at the school. They seemed tight off the court, too. They were girls who genuinely liked one another and remained immune to petty spats and personal jealousies.

Three of the starters attended the same church at the Wasilla Assembly of God and had attended a weeklong lakeside powwow that was part sports camp, part religious retreat. If this team was going to become a faith-based high school basketball team, so much the better. Any gathering of kids who maintained a genuine faith in the miracle of the resurrection was also fully capable in believing in the miraculous possibility of winning a state championship against extremely long odds. The fact that several of the girls were tall and talented basketball players did not hurt a bit, either.

This was a sharp contrast to Teeguarden's inaugural season, when some of the players were not sure whether they wanted to shoot hoops or lead cheers. Now the coach had been presented with a well-rounded collection of competitors who were polished and fundamentally solid, thanks to Jerry Yates's tutoring at the junior high school. Some were exceptionally tall, some were strong enough to defeat a grown man at arm wrestling (if they had wanted to), and a couple of others could jump like antelopes.

After its rocky beginning when Teeguarden had

become the coach, the program had started to blossom. The player who had told Teeguarden, after that Christmastime drubbing at Kodiak seasons earlier, that the only way to improve was to compete against the best, had been dead right. The program had evolved to the extent that while the Warriors weren't quite the best, they were among the contenders. Twice the Warriors had advanced to the state tournament in Anchorage, and two seasons before had fallen in the championship game against East—with more than twice Wasilla's enrollment—in Anchorage.

The program had improved, Teeguarden thought, not because of any real expertise he'd gained as a coach—the coach who "didn't know anything" when he accepted the job. The success initiative was based on an identity factor that he'd instilled in his players. Teeguarden started playing the underdog card, and with that, the Warriors had begun to rake in some chips.

His definition of "underdog," and the interpretation that he pitched to the girls, had nothing to do with talent deficiencies. The Teeguarden approach amounted to the big-city versus small-town culture clash. He convinced his kids that the players at the Anchorage schools basically regarded the Wasillans as an assembly of hicks from the sticks. It was true, too. Anchorage, with its nondescript downtown area and overall dismal architectural tableau, could never be confused with San Francisco, or Fresno for that matter, as a cosmopolitan entity. Even into the 1980s, Anchorage retained a bit of the feel of its old tent-city heritage from the gold rush era. Despite that, many Anchorage residents looked down their runny noses at the Wasillans, who became known as Valley Trash.

Teeguarden loved the concept. "Valley Trash" was a put-down that resonated among the Mat-Su natives to the extent that many bought T-shirts emblazoned with the term. It was a source of community pride. The girls certainly grasped the message, and soon they took to the court wearing a sizable chip on their shoulder, particularly when taking on a team from Anchorage or the larger schools on the touristy and prosperous Kenai Peninsula, where oil and gas production was booming.

The coach stressed the theme at the beginning of fall practice and throughout the season. When they took trips down to Anchorage, he'd remind the team, "They think the yokels are coming into town, riding in the back of a turnip truck. But we're good enough to run with the big dogs! Now let's go show them what good team basketball really is!"

To Teeguarden, it was the easiest of all sells. "And it worked," he would reflect years later, "because it wasn't a con."

So, at the advent of the 1981–1982 campaign, Teeguarden pondered what might lie ahead as he pursued a regular season schedule cluttered with teams that were the best in Alaska. Three high schools in Anchorage—East, Robert Service, and Bartlett—would begin their seasons as the betting favorites to take the girls state title. Two schools from frigid Fairbanks, Monroe Catholic and Lathrop, were going to be difficult to beat. Outside the larger cities, Kenai, Kodiak, and Cordova had always been good and figured to be again. He realized that this group had two things working in its favor—the chip-on-the-shoulder gambit, and the reassurance that the team was constituted of stable, high-character kids. The point of concern that the girls shared involved something that they did have in common with the kids who existed on The Outside. That was the future. High school and the games that came with it would be over soon enough. What then? Stay or leave. The notion of leaving home and leaving the state to go off to school was far more profound to Alaskan kids than to high school seniors in most other parts of the United States because the cost of such missions of discovery was prohibitive for so many families. The natural instinct for many kids was to leave home and explore, but for Alaskans, that meant a lonely journey into the unknown, where the manifestations of culture shock would be inevitable.

But Teeguarden knew this group had the capacity to focus on the game of basketball and not any conflicts in their off-the-court lives. What concerned Teeguarden as the season approached was a shortage of actual tangibles. If most of the players had one thing in common, it was a lack of actual varsity game experience. The key operatives from the previous team that had fallen one game shy of the state championship were graduated and gone. The strength of that unit was that it consisted of skilled backcourt players. The guard play had been exceptional, not just quick but fast as well.

The 1981–1982 ensemble, if it were to succeed, would have to rely upon a whole different skill set from the year before.

Teeguarden realized the current group had good size, and it was not bereft of athletic talent. The stomp-butt girls from Jerry Yates's excellent program at the junior high had matured into excellent high school athletes.

Heyde Kohring was a senior now, and had finally stopped growing at six foot two. The awkward beanpole from junior high days had developed into a lean and agile player with a good shooting touch. In 3-on-3 practice drills, Teeguarden had been especially encouraged with Heyde's capacity to work both ends of the court and her innate capacity to utilize her height advantage. Her personality was emerging as well. During her sophomore and junior seasons, Teeguarden could not recall Heyde ever saying a word.

The size factor that Heyde contributed was nicely enhanced by Wanda Strutko, a sturdy six-footer who was not timid about jumping into the fray underneath the hoop when elbows were flying. And Strutko was strong, somebody who would not be pushed around by the combat that happened under the basket. She was gifted not only with stamina but, even for her size, amazing jumping ability. One drawback: Wanda was only a sophomore.

Jackie Conn was not as tall as Heyde or Wanda, but superior from the standpoint of strength and overall athletic skills. Conn was one of the best high school girl shot-putters in the whole state. Better yet, Jackie had keen basketball instincts, quickly picking up the aspects of strategies that would be employed in game situations. In key moments of tight games, Jackie Conn was the one player that the coach wanted to have the ball in her hands. Shoot. Pass. Drive to the basket, no matter what the situation, Jackie always, every time, made the right choice and in the category of basketball smarts, she was the class valedictorian. After one early practice, Teeguarden would tell his assistant, Cordell Randall, "The thing I really like about Jackie is that she is one of those players who *just gets it*." During game action, Conn wore a perpetual scowl on her face that certain opponents found intimidating.

While the prospects for the upcoming season would be, if nothing else, rich in uncertainty, as the preseason workouts progressed, Teeguarden realized that Kohring, Strutko, and Conn would, at least in the box scores, serve as the

Warriors' Big Three. He also realized that in basketball, at the championship level, three alone wouldn't hack it. It took five.

Karen Bush showed enough in practice to earn one of the two remaining spots in the starting lineup. At first glance, there was nothing in her game to remind the on-looker of Magic Johnson, necessarily. What impressed Tee-guarden most about Bush was that she had been successful in track, running what was then the 440-yard dash. Whether it was run by boys or girls, Teeguarden knew that the 440 was no place for creampuffs. That was a competition that required natural speed, staying power, and most impor-tant, guts. The more Teeguarden saw of Bush, the more he was confident that he could win with her in the lineup. Bush had developed a nifty jump shot from the 12- to 15-foot range, and that was an added bonus that would become vital against the zone defenses that opposing teams would employ against the Warriors' big girls.

The coach sensed that he had some of the basic ingre-dients for a pretty good basketball recipe. For the thing to work, in order to perhaps amount to something special, if not exceptional, the ultimate requirement would be an effec-tive point guard. All of the size and scoring ability that came with the Big Three of Kohring, Strutko, and Conn would go untapped and wasted unless there was someone to feed them the ball.

More than that, Wasilla would also be facing an assembly of opposing teams that earned their living on the concept of the full-court press—all game long. That was especially true of East High School in Anchorage, the top-ranked girls team in the state, an outfit that took to the court and applied the press like a pack of angry and starving wolves. The point guard was the player required to be gifted with uncanny vision and cool wits, to handle both the physical and mental demands of the relentless press. This was the cog that during the long run of the season would be the determinant of whether the Warriors would live or die.

If Teeguarden was certain of anything, it was the player on the point who would have to drive the bus. She was the daughter of the Wasilla High School track coach, and Teeguarden felt that the titles of a couple of pretty good Hollywood motion pictures could be used to describe this girl: *True Grit* and *The Right Stuff.*

Not overwhelmingly gifted with raw basketball talent, the player had labored relentlessly to refine the skills that she did possess, had learned the basic elements as a kid in something known as the Wasilla Little Dribblers program and later had even traveled to some place called George West, Texas, to participate in a summertime hoops camp for boys and girls. During her junior season, she had struggled to get much playing time, since the talent and experience and the strength of the team was based on the guard play.

At midseason, rather than let a promising player sit idle on the bench, Teeguarden assigned her to the Wasilla junior varsity squad, where she could play full time and refine her skills. She took the news hard, he could tell, but she didn't complain, and she worked like a coal miner in an effort to get better.

Now a senior and for the first time poised to get real varsity playing time, the girl had become a master of the no-look pass, and teammates who weren't always alert would likely find the ball bouncing off the side of their heads.

She would contribute an element of poise and maturity to the Warriors' squad, plus leadership skills based on example and not artificial rah-rah. Her teammates readily detected that, and while she might have in fact been the least talented of the five starters, the Warriors elected her co-captain the week before the season opener. So what if her grade point average might exceed her points-scored total in certain games. If anybody had earned her way into the starting lineup through sheer will, unceasing work, and raw determination, it was this girl.

She was tougher than the filet mignon that they served at Mel's Diner. This was Sarah Heath. Two years hence, Sarah would be named Miss Congeniality at the conclusion of the Miss Alaska pageant, but she was anything but congenial when the action got underway on the hardwood.

What Don Teeguarden ascertained as the preseason

wound down and the opening game quickly approached was that this team certainly offered the potential to become a winner. He also remembered a quote he'd read a decade earlier from a college football coach named Darrell Royal: "Potential means you ain't done it yet." And a major league baseball manager, Whitey Herzog, had said: "Potential is what gets you fired."

Still, this largely untested group had sampled success in a huge way during their junior varsity seasons as sophomores. Heath, Kohring, Conn, and Bush all performed on a team that posted an eighteen and one record. They had beaten JV teams from all over the state: Anchorage, Fairbanks, Kenai, Homer, Seward, Valdez, Cordova, Palmer, Delta, and Kodiak. Wasilla's swarming defense had limited the Cordova team to three field *attempts* in an entire half. So it was with a sense of tempered optimism that Don Teeguarden stood poised to sic his Valley Trash upon the foes that lurked on the icy trails that stretched ahead.

Chapter 5

Since the birth of the American nation, the average man, good old Joe Sixpack, has worked and strived to ward off the ultimate symbol of adversity known as the wolf at the door. In Alaska, though, the concern is more in regards to the moose at the door, and there is nothing symbolic about that.

Those boorish neighbors wearing antler racks that measured out as the approximate size of a small pontoon plane were commonly known to barge right into the home, unannounced, uninvited, and they'd take the food right off the kitchen counter and not even say, "Please."

Chuck Heath, father of Sarah Heath, point guard of the Wasilla Warriors, has a photo he took of a moose that was attempting a home invasion on hoofs through the rear entry of his household in search of a brunch-time snack. The expression on the moose's face did not seem all that cordial. On one occasion, Chuck counted eleven of the audacious creatures standing in his yard.

In other parts of the world, cultural diversity hasn't always worked that well. Alaska is different. In Alaska, people routinely and casually coexist with those of different skin colors and spiritual beliefs . . . a sampling of those being the brown bear, the black bear, the caribou, the beaver, the porcupine, the coyote, the lynx, the salmon, the Beluga whale, the harbor seal, the red fox, the wolf, and the ever-present moose; not to mention the Aleutian Tern, the Northern Hawk Owl, the rock piper, the Pacific Loon, the Boreal Chickadee, the Sandhill Crane, the Spruce Grouse, and the soaring bald eagle.

These various species and the humankind that pass among them have their occasional spats, but mostly they all tend to be politically Independent Conservative and their mindset is one that says, "Hey, we're all in this together, so why can't we just get along?" That was the attitude that attracted Chuck Heath to this splendidly rustic venue in the first place. If ever a person and place were meant for one another, it was Heath and the state of Alaska. To know Chuck Heath is to immediately comprehend the origin of the spunk and energy that his long-distance running, basketball-playing daughter had displayed since early childhood.

Heath's point of origin was Sandpoint, Idaho, a setting in its own right that was scarcely the domain of prissy idlers, layabouts, or fops with a passion for fashion. In 1888, a twenty-nine-year-old journalist named Teddy Roosevelt passed through Sandpoint and proclaimed it "as rough and tumble a town as I have ever seen." Sandpoint, situated at the base of the vertical Idaho panhandle that extends upward to the Canadian border, had been a logging town until the logs ran out sometime during the Depression. What was left was an assortment of what were known as stump ranches, but the jaw-busting spirit of the lumberjack lived on in Sandpoint, where a man's best friend might be his ax handle.

By natural inclination, Heath was a born sportsman. Not just the hunter-fisherman kind of sportsman, although there was plenty of that in his DNA, but also the ball sports kind of sportsman, and the track and field sports, and most any other form of athletic enterprise that involved competition. Geared to those kinds of enthusiasms, Heath was ordained with a lucky childhood. His father, by profession, was a sports photographer, and a gifted one, who worked at first for newspapers and then as a freelancer based out of Sandpoint.

The bulk of the elder Heath's portfolio contained work for outdoor publications of the *Field & Stream* genre, and as a kid Chuck tagged along with his dad on various assignments, and that put the boy in proximity with people who knew what they were doing, and he paid attention to their habits and work ethic. Also, his father's job enabled him to meet an assortment of celebrities from the sports world.

To this day, two of his most prized treasures remain on display in the hallway of his Wasilla home. They are photos taken by his father in which Chuck at age seven posed with Primo Carnera and Jim Jeffries, both former heavyweight boxing champions of the world. The expression on the boy's face looks like something from a Norman Rockwell illustration on the cover of *The Saturday Evening Post*. The gleam in his eye so keenly captured by his father's camera lens presents the unmistakable portrait of a happy and rewarding childhood.

Chuck Heath believes his fortunes were further enhanced by the appearance in his life of another man—Cotton Barlow. From a personality standpoint, Barlow was anything but the gentle and understanding father figure. Barlow was the head football coach at Sandpoint High, and the Sandpoint Bulldogs were well-known throughout the Northwest during the early Fifties—well-known and feared because that was the way that Cotton Barlow demanded it.

Prisoners chained together and swinging picks on rock piles, on a day-to-day basis, had more fun than Barlow's Bulldogs football team during practice. Chuck Heath remembers the white, sticky substance, like Elmer's glue, that coated his mouth and tongue during the workouts. Water was taboo. Water was for sissies. Looking back on his Cotton Barlow days and his apprenticeship amid the flames of Hades, Chuck Heath reflects, "It's a wonder that he didn't kill us all."

Barlow offered a simple motivational message to his boys before they took the field on game nights: "I don't really care about the final score, but if you don't beat those guys to a (expletive) pulp, then God help you all in practice on Monday." That spiritual pepper-upper seemed to work wonders, and in Heath's four seasons on the football team at Sandpoint, the Bulldogs lost a total of four games. During those four seasons, Heath had a friend and teammate whose later gridiron exploits reflected the style of play of Barlow's Bulldogs.

He was Jerry Kramer, an athlete who provided the living definition of the concept of "hard-nosed" and who went on to play football for the University of Idaho Vandals, and then, more famously, with the Green Bay Packers during the seasons when they were the absolute scourge of the National Football League. Kramer, the offensive guard, became the linchpin of the Packers famed power sweep. The name and memory of Green Bay coach Vince Lombardi and his mantra that went, "Fatigue makes cowards of us all," resounds as the harshest, most brutal and demanding despot in the history of football.

In Jerry Kramer's thinking, Vince Lombardi—and his tortuous "grass drills" that were conducted while professional football players puked and passed out—was Captain Kangaroo when compared to Cotton Barlow. On the deciding final play of the so-called Ice Bowl game, played at a chill factor that measured about minus 90, Jerry Kramer applied the most famous block in the annals of the sport. He jumped the count by the nanosecond he needed to get leverage on Dallas Cowboy defensive tackle Jethro Pugh, and without Kramer's heroics, Bart Starr would mostly certainly have been stopped short of the goal line on his quarterback sneak that won the NFL champion game and propelled the Pack to its cakewalk victory over the Oakland Raiders in the Super Bowl.

Kramer, who played the sport with such ferocious intensity that he would undergo what must be a league career record of twenty-two surgeries on various portions of his beaten-up body, must have been inspired—in the back of his mind—to make that critical Ice Bowl block for the appeasement of Cotton Barlow, who he imagined must have been somewhere watching.

Chuck Heath was watching, too, on television at his own home in Alaska, where he would locate himself for the rest of his lifetime beginning fours year earlier.

During college, Heath decided that he wanted to become a schoolteacher, believing that he had a lot to offer kids, plus the knack of presenting course material in a fashion that they'd understand and maybe even enjoy. He chose to move to Alaska from Idaho for a couple of reasons. First, he'd visited the state on a few hunting and fishing adventures and was naturally enchanted by the place, and second, because of the rigors presented by living there, teaching salaries were a little higher than in Idaho. So he took a chance. With his wife, Sally—a brown-eyed beauty who would eventually come to enjoy the quest of wildlife maybe even more than her husband—and their two little kids, they embarked on a pursuit of life—for better or worse, richer or poorer—in the daunting kingdom of the Yukon.

Right away, Chuck and Sally knew they were entering a lifestyle that offered few, actually more closer to none, of the conveniences conventionally associated with the ease and prosperity of the American Dream. Heath's first job was in Skagway, in the southeast portion of the state, on the outskirts of the Tongass National Forest and not far from the original site of the Klondike gold rush. If Heath had been lured to Alaska by the well-known call of the wild, then he could not have selected a better location than Skagway, which had been the actual setting for the unforgettable novel of the same name. During the gold rush era, it was said that the name of the town Skagway could have more appropriately renamed Scoundrel City.

The place was overrun with greed-crazy opportunists like Soapy Smith, an entrepreneur who ran the Western Union office in 1896. He would charge prospectors $5 to send a telegram anywhere in the world, and that went on for nearly three years before it was determined that Skagway was not equipped with telegraph service. Eventually, he would be shot. But Soapy and his ilk were all dead and gone by the time the Heath family entered the town that lay well beyond the city limits of civilization.

In the winter months, Skagway stood out as a poster child for abject isolation. The only thing more difficult than getting in was getting out.

After a year, Heath got out of Skagway, not because of the inherent hardships that place presented, but because Chuck decided he would obtain a graduate degree and the only thing that place had to offer was the Skagway Ph.D. That stood for post-hole digger. In order to get his master's in teaching, Heath would have to pursue that at the University of Alaska at Anchorage.

He relocated the family to the Mat-Su Valley, within commuting distance of the university while continuing his teaching work, first in Chugiak, and finally, at Wasilla. The Wasilla-to-Anchorage run, and return trip, during the long ripping cold of the dark months could be something of an intimidating journey. A flat tire or mechanical break-down on what was then a two-lane road could be a life-threatening event. Heath appeased himself by resorting to the Cotton Barlow outlook—concentrate on the positives.

In those days, at least he wouldn't have to cope with much traffic.

His sense of unflagging determination would pay off in the form of the master's degree and the stable job that came with it. Heath landed a position teaching English at Iditarod Elementary in Wasilla, where Sally worked as a school secretary and the couple was able to purchase a home that was large enough to house a family that had grown to four children.

In addition to English and social studies classes, Chuck was soon appointed to teach a grade-school class that would be far more vital to the kids of Alaska than anything within the textbooks containing the basics of the Three Rs: the course that was called Bear and Moose Safety.

The fundamentals of the study involved how to react when attacked by the various categories of bear. In a run-in with a brown or black bear, it was important to remember that the creature was probably growing cranky at mealtime and determined to eat you alive. Poke the creature's eyes out, if possible; do whatever it takes to escape. Of course, that was easier said than accomplished. These enormous creatures can run thirty-five miles an hour.

A bear joke often told in Alaskan barrooms went like this: Two campers watch as the black bear approaches. One camper quickly puts on a pair of track shoes. "You don't actually think you can outrun that bear, do you?" says his companion. "I don't need to outrun the bear," answers the guy in the track shoes. "I just need to outrun *you*."

Heath would show the kids a horrifying photo, a ghastly thing that showed a man who had not avoided the dinner-time proclivities of an ursine marauder. What remained looked like a turkey carcass three days after Thanksgiving. All that was left was the victim's hiking boots. In the latter years of teaching his Bear and Moose Safety class, one of the students would show Heath an amusing cartoon. Two brown bears are talking and one says to the other: "Those people snacks really make me feel good. They're loaded with antidepressants."

Now, a grizzly attack, Heath would explain, presented a different tactic. Grizzlies go after humans not as a culinary objective, but out of sheer misanthropic meanness, an act of domination. So the idea is to play dead. There was a recommended posture for that, and Heath would stand in front of the class and demonstrate, placing both hands behind his head. If Plan B was called into play, if you're right-handed, try to fend the bear off with your left arm, and vice versa, because even if you survive, you're likely to lose the arm.

The teacher knew all too well that the strategy was not foolproof. A person who experienced a grizzly attack and lived to tell the tale had told him: "The thing tossed me around like a rag doll, and let me tell you, it's hard to play dead when you are flying through the air." Heath could count six acquaintances who had had a bad bear encounter. Four had survived.

Heath kept a list that a friend had given him that he was tempted to present to his class, but never did:

Ten Things to Do When You Run into a Wild Alaskan Bear

1. Grab your camera.
2. If you have no camera, make a quick sketch. (Bears love to pose!)
3. Roll yourself into a three-inch diameter ball.
4. Perform the death scene from *Romeo and Juliet*. (Bears love good theater!)
5. Try to look like a brussels sprout and not a steak.
6. Run the mile in thirty seconds.
7. Hold your breath until you puff up like a large marshmallow.
8. Do your best impersonation of the Hulk.
9. Try not to act as appetizing as you look.
10. Stay inside and watch TV instead of going out for a hike.

The main point of emphasis of the course was that in Alaska, three times as many people were killed by moose than bear. People did not have to venture into the wilderness to come face-to-face with a moose, either. They roamed the streets of every city, town, and village in the whole state.

"The moose might look lovable enough on Saturday morning kiddie cartoons," Heath would explain to the class, "but they're cantankerous and dangerous. It's not those big antlers that they use in attacks, it's the long legs. The angry moose will butt you down and stomp you to death." He'd witnessed such an event that took place right down in Anchorage, on the campus of the university. Some kids had been throwing snowballs at a moose that became agitated. That same moose then went after some old man and did a flamenco dance on his torso until he was dead.

Heath could never be sure exactly how beneficial his lectures in the class had been, but he'd never lost a student in wildlife combat, so he must have been doing something good. His teaching abilities were well-known and well-thought-of in the Wasilla schools, to the extent that Heath would receive a call from the principal at the high school. The principal offered a moonlighting opportunity. Would Chuck be interested in coaching the cross-country team?

Like Don Teeguarden later, when the girls basketball coaching proposition was extended, Chuck Heath's first-hand knowledge of the fine art of distance running was absolutely nil. Just as Teeguarden did, he accepted, knowing that he would have to learn the tricks of the trade strictly through on-the-job training.

The distance running program at Wasilla amounted to an exercise that was one step below mediocre. That was because, in Heath's estimation, the coaching was substandard, administered part time by indifferent teachers who knew nothing about running and could not have cared less.

In the process of accomplishing something better, Heath would first read every book on distance running that he could lay his hands on. He was pleased to learn that there were quite a few. What proved even more instructive was material contained in the pages of *Runner's World* magazine. He subscribed at once, located back issues, and studied them from cover to cover, and if that wasn't enough, he watched instructional films.

According to his diploma, Chuck Heath was a master teacher, and his driving ambition had been to demonstrate that in real life. In addition to the book information, Heath decided it was essential to not just teach the sport, but he had to begin running as well. Mind control was key. How could he impart anything of use to his runners in that regard if he didn't experience it himself?

Heath had been a high school sprinter at Sandpoint High School, and set a school record in the hundred-yard dash that had lasted for several years. The longer distances presented a whole different discipline. Heath decided to run along with the kids during practice—a situation he approached with a somewhat dubious outlook because at the time he was a smoker.

Soon enough, Heath joined a group of Alaskan elite distance runners—not out of a spirit of competition; he wasn't yet in their league—but to pick their brains on anything and everything he could harvest from the pros. What he learned mostly was that successfully competitive distance runners came with lean bodies and excellent brain synapses. It pleased him no end to take his Wasilla boys and girls team to a cross-country meet on a bus that contained among the twenty-two runners, twenty-two honor students.

After two years tutoring the cross-country athletes, Heath took over the entire track program at Wasilla High. He liked to conduct indoor meets, on the second floor track that encircled the gym, and was often seen prowling the crowded hallways of the school with a pistol, a .22 caliber luger, strapped to his hip. That was his starter's gun, loaded with blanks, but he liked to think it offered a message to the kids. Don't mess with Chuck, a man with a hawk-like beak who somewhat resembled the warrior that adorned the front side of the high school.

The only thing that set him apart was the sense of compassion that radiated from his eyes, a quality distinctly missing on the image of the bad news brave.

In 1981, Chuck Heath's school year had gotten off to a good start. His girls cross-country team had won the meet conducted at the Settler's Bay golf course that clinched the regional championship. In cross-country, the team with the lowest score won and Wasilla had nosed out Kodiak for the title, 42–43. "That was no cakewalk," Chuck Heath told the local paper. He said he was proud of his top finisher, Deena Ludington. "When she came out for the team two years ago, Deena was a tiny, wimpy little thing and I didn't think she'd stick it out. She doesn't hoot and holler, but the other girls realize how she has improved and look up to her and follow her example."

Another top finisher was Heath's daughter, Sarah, who'd edged out a Kodiak runner for sixth place out of a field of about one hundred. Reverse that order of finish and Kodiak, not Wasilla, would have won the meet. In his post-race interview, Chuck didn't mention Sarah. When it came to coaching his own daughter, Heath pushed Sarah more than the rest, rode her hard at times, to the extent that one of his runners once approached him, smiled, and said, "I'm glad I'm not Sarah."

With the conclusion of the cross-country season, Heath's preoccupation turned to girls basketball. Now Chuck Heath the coach had become Chuck Heath the avid fan. He watched and cheered for Sarah and teammates at all of the home games, and most of the nearby road contests. Heath,

working and playing twenty hours a day in land that provided five hours of sunlight, was experiencing life at its
fullest.

When he wasn't teaching grade school Bear and Moose
Safety and rooting for the basketball girls, Chuck was up
early and running several miles in the darkness amid late
autumn temperatures that were well-below freezing and getting lower and meaner by the day. He had a surprise in store
for the community. That coming spring, Chuck Heath—
the reformed smoker who learned to run by jogging along
with his cross-country kids—was going to compete in the
Boston Marathon.

Chapter 6

In Wasilla, when October comes, so, too, does the wind, roaring down off the Bering Sea, along with the snow. By November, the thermometer rarely tiptoed above the freezing mark, and the idea of 20 below, on some occasions, was not out of the question. As the tyranny of the approaching arctic winter made its relentless advance into Mat-Su Valley with the advent of November, a headline warned residents that **NORTHERN LIGHTS WREAK HAVOC WITH ELECTRIC LINES**. The accompanying story said that intense electrical currents caused disruptions in the power circuits. Just one more thing to worry about.

By this time of year, the sun was making phantom appearances, never directly overhead, scooting around the horizon like an egg yolk on a plate. Year-round residents were asking each other, "Have you something to do?" Here in the darkness, everybody vitally needed a diversion, a hobby. Without that, the devil presented himself in the tacky disguise of a liquor bottle, and those who succumbed to that ruse soon presented a side to their personalities that was darker than the sky.

If nothing else, a person might enroll in an adult education class. Wasilla's Doug Fesler, for instance, was offering a night course in how to survive an avalanche. More cheerfully, an ad in the newspaper in Palmer, Wasilla's sister town, offered this remedy to the wintertime blues:

> Are you suffering from Lackadancia? Symptoms—bored at social functions. The doldrums. Don't take Geritol when you can take this one-time special $10 offer for $75 worth of lessons at the Fred Astaire Dance Studio.

On the same page as the dance studio promo, a short article on the Metro page reminded the readers that life around there was not a typical episode of *Father Knows Best*.

> James Sullivan reported that a drinking companion had robbed him of $15 and assaulted him. Troopers said events in the case are unclear. Both the alleged assailant and the victim have left the area.

A cynic might have supposed that the victim skipped town because he no longer had the dough to take his tango lessons. Hardship also came to those Alaskans who were anything but patrons of the jug, but living advocates of clean living and straight thinking. Dick Marsh, a pastor at the Pioneer Peak Baptist Church in Butte, had been out in the woods walking up a slope and pursuing his cold weather hobby, elk hunting, when he heard a noise from behind that he said, "Sounded like a steam engine. A large brown bear was on me in less than two seconds, about ten feet away. I screamed, tripped over a log, and turned a backward somersault."

Then Marsh did what any resourceful preacher man would do. He took his .243 lever-action Sako-Finnwolf rifle and fired from the hip. His first shot nailed the bear in the chest, and two more shots finished the creature that measured nine feet four inches from nose to tail, for good. The following Sunday, from his pulpit, Pastor Marsh offered his congregation a prayer that went: "O Lord, you delivered Daniel from the lion's den. You delivered Jonah from the belly of a whale and the Hebrew children from the fiery earth, so the Good Book does declare. But Lord, if you can't help me, for goodness sakes, don't help that bear."

Events like those reinforced Don Teeguarden's notion that an activity like girls basketball, for all its occasional tribulation, might serve as the most practical outlet of all. It was trying at times, but nobody ever got drunk, robbed, or eaten alive. The season opener against Palmer that was traditionally held on the Wednesday night before Thanksgiving was rapidly approaching, so he keyed up the intensity of the practice sessions.

At the conclusion of a workout two days prior to the opener, a participant in a scrimmage approached the coach, pointed to his sophomore post player Wanda Strutko, and said, "God almighty! She just beat the living crap outta me!"

The complainant was not one of Teeguarden's second-string girls, but rather his six-foot-three-inch tall assistant coach and right-hand man, Cordell Randall. Teeguarden had put Randall into dress rehearsal before the opener to add some physicality to the practice. Teeguarden was pleased to hear that report, and Randall in reality had been happy to deliver it. The only thing rougher than basketball practice was cheerleading practice, which took place at the other side of the gym. One afternoon, one of the cheerleaders fell off a pyramid and broke her neck.

Randall, who, unlike Teeguarden, had some actual basketball playing background, had joined the Wasilla girls program the season before and quickly became an integral part of the operation. He was a coach's kid from California and a pretty good high school player, with height and court skills to play both guard and small forward. What was notable about Randall's high school career was that he played for the school on the 89,000-acre Hoopa (pronounced hoopah) Indian reservation, 300 miles north of San Francisco, where his father had been a teacher. The Hoopa tribe is recognized as California's original humanity, predating even the motion picture industry.

Young Cordell absorbed quite a few elements of the Hoopa culture, including participating in the tribe's Sacred Jump Dance. Occasionally, he would join a team for a pickup game in a sport called *tossel*, which involved heaving two heavy wooden blocks, attached by rope, over the opponents' goal. There were no rules that barred any physical defensive tactics whatsoever. What Randall remembered about tossel was that "it was probably the only game rougher than Russian roulette."

Finishing high school, Randall had received one scholarship offer (from the University of Alaska at Fairbanks), and he jumped at the opportunity. He understood that he was in all likelihood plunging headfirst into a life-altering situation. Randall fought back tears when his parents put him on a plane at the San Francisco airport, where he told them *"Nuniwhtsis-te,"* which in the Hoopa dialect means, "Good-bye. I will see you again." Despite having girded himself for an excursion into the mysterious unknown, Cordell Randall had not fully appreciated what the routine of life in Fairbanks might actually entail.

In the Anchorage and Mat-Su Valley region, winters were cold, but the climate in this area amounted to sweater weather compared to the Fairbanks ordeal. When Randall described life in Fairbanks, the operative word, and he used it a lot, was "brutal." He learned not to breathe too deeply, because the air seared his lungs.

The good thing about playing basketball at the Fairbanks school was that the team traveled a lot, probably logging more air miles during the season than any college team in the United States. They traveled to various locations all along the Pacific Coast, sometimes down into Southern California, and they flew to Hawaii. But always, there was a return flight. Randall might have been uncertain about returning to this gelid hell on earth until fate had intervened.

Cordell Randall's college basketball tenure had coincided with the Vietnam era, and when the draft lottery took place, among the young men in the entire American Selective Service System, he drew number 16. Right away, Randall received a cheery communication from Uncle Sam that informed him where and when to report in the event that he left school or was ever placed on academic probation. Motivated like no other time in his life, Randall hit the court and hit the books with an enthusiasm that surprised even him.

After his college graduation and free from the obligation of a possible all-expense paid trip to the jungles in Southeast Asia, he returned to a more conventional kind of life, teaching school in California. Yet a strange thing had happened to him as he completed his four years in Fairbanks. He'd begun to like the place. He would never adjust fully to 50 below temperatures, but the landscape and the people who came with it offered an element of undeniable appeal.

During a telephone conversation with a college friend with connections, Randall learned that he could secure employment working on the construction of the Trans-Alaska Pipeline. If the prospect of doing that wasn't exotic enough, the salary certainly was, and soon lanky Cordell Randall was back in the Great Northland. He worked as a construction camp maintenance supervisor. The pay, he thought, was stupendous.

But as the months passed, his contentment level diminished. This time, it was not the raging winter winds that got him down, nor the demands of the work. It was simply an overpowering sense of isolation, a separation from family and friends, that was becoming harder and harder to withstand. Also, opportunities for reasonable female companionship that did not involve women from the hospitality industry were not easy to find.

He was not ready to leave Alaska, though, and settled for the compromise of a school system job in Palmer, coordinating home school parents and serving as offensive assistant coach on the football team. Like most towns in Alaska, there were no places in the Lower 48 that were quite like it. In August, Palmer was the site of the Alaskan State

Fair, an event that brought some entries worthy of *Ripley's Believe It or Not!*

Because of the ceaseless summer sunshine, plant life does otherworldly things: carrots become the size of small trees; potatoes grow as big as Volkswagen Beetles. This stuff was commonplace at the Palmer fair. Want to see a big head of cabbage? How about a seventy-nine-and-a-half pounder? These specimens are not grown to be eaten, but for show purposes only.

Palmer and Wasilla, because of their proximity—being just eight miles apart—were known, if not as Twin Cities, then Twin Towns, although the twins were not identical. The situation was ideal for a healthy sort of sibling rivalry that was best manifested in the athletic competitions between the two high schools. It was a good-natured taunt-the-other-team kind of rivalry that never became acrimonious enough to lead to a postgame rumble in the parking lot. On frequent occasions, after the competition had ended, players from Wasilla and Palmer might socialize together in a pizza restaurant.

Teeguarden's counterpart at Palmer was Ralph Sallee, who had been a promising pitcher in the Los Angeles Dodgers minor league chain until Sallee's arm went bad, and the injury eventually charted Sallee's arrival in Alaska. When he learned of Cordell Randall's college hoops background at Fairbanks, Sallee quickly brought him on board to help him coach the girls.

One of the remote axioms in sports is that bad arms make good coaches, and that was the case with Ralph Sallee. Before the launching of the Don Teeguarden era at Wasilla, Palmer's team, the Moose, had never lost to the Warriors. Once Teeguarden's program had gotten up and running, though, Palmer never beat Wasilla again.

Cordell Randall enjoyed his tenure in Palmer. But in Teeguarden, he saw an exceptional coach, a "helluva coach" in his estimation, and when Teeguarden approached him with the notion of coming over to Wasilla to fill an opening, Randall was eager to accept, and pleased with the opportunity to work with what he regarded as a great coach in a program that was becoming great as well. When he told Sallee that he was jumping ship and moving to Wasilla, the Palmer coach could scarcely begrudge his choice.

In competing against Wasilla, Randall had been impressed with the calm, even serene, nature of Teeguarden's courtside manner. Never, not once, had he seen Teeguarden raise his voice when talking to his players, much less yell at one. Rarely, in fact, had he seen the coach of the Warriors even yell at an official.

The Teeguarden–Randall relationship had meshed well, and the assistant had played an active role in rigging the sails of the 1981–1982 Warriors' frigate that was about to leave port.

Randall was hot to trot for the regular season. Since he wasn't head coach, the pressures were not as suffocating as Teeguarden's—as long as the assistant didn't have to drive the bus. That experience, which had happened the season before, had been the most nerve-racking event of his entire life, piloting a group of kids along an icy highway. Randall was grateful when the transmission broke and a replacement bus and driver were summoned to rescue the group.

For years, Randall had heard tales from the days of Alaska's high school basketball past and the hardships of travel that the coaches and players had to withstand. It had been commonplace for teams to journey to hostile locales aboard fishing boats. Winning on the road was hard, not so much because of the tough environment, but because the visitors arrived for the games on wobbly sea legs, suffering from the after-effects of seasickness.

On one legendary occasion, a team from the Sheldon Jackson boarding school got so sick on a voyage across the Chatham Strait to Petersburg that the players vomited into their equipment bags rather than befoul the floor of their sleeping area inside the boat. And they went on to win the game, because no player on the Petersburg squad would come close to guarding a Sheldon Jackson player because of the stench emanating from the uniforms.

Whether that actually occurred or not, after the school bus incident Randall would consider himself an authority on the hair-raising facets of traveling to the games. On road trips, the kids would bed down on the opposing team's gym floor, in sleeping bags, and dine on school cafeteria fare.

Assistant Coach Randall especially enjoyed the journey to Kodiak, usually the longest hop on the Wasilla schedule, where the school provided the best oatmeal cookies he'd ever eaten. He obtained the recipe and learned that the real secret was not overbaking the cookies.

As far as the actual basketball was concerned, more than Teeguarden, Randall was optimistic about the team's chances to make a deep run toward the state title. One reason had been his scrimmage experience. He'd found trying to move around Jackie Conn was like, as he put it to Teeguarden, "running into a brick wall." Whereas Strutko, the sophomore who had elbowed him into submission, was "strong as an ox."

Oh, and the point guard. Randall liked her, too. During her junior season, Sarah Heath had constantly pleaded with and cajoled the assistant coach for playing time. "Just give me a chance. That's all I want," had been Sarah's oft-repeated refrain. Now she was finally getting it, and Randall, who'd been around, was dead certain that the dark-haired girl wearing Number 22 would make the most of it. Finally, the curtain was about to rise for the grand opening of the

1981–1982 season. The mood of the players was one of unrestrained elation. After the extensive hours of afternoon practice session, they could scarcely wait to begin their five-month adventure into competition, road trips, and fellowship that would generate a lifetime of memories. Teeguarden's primary concern was that his team might be *too* ready.

The Wasilla gym was jammed on the Wednesday night of the pre-Thanksgiving opener against the Palmer Moose. In high school girls basketball, each quarter opened with a jump ball at midcourt and during the final of practice, Teeguarden had worked on set plays from the tip-off. Heyde Kohring, the tallest player on the court, would make the jump and tip the ball to Strutko, strategically positioned at the back of the circle. Kohring would tip the ball high enough that Strutko would have to jump for it. Strutko would then feed the ball to Jackie Conn, streaking toward the basket.

When the game started, the play worked exactly as the girls had practiced and with the season exactly four seconds old, the Warriors led 2–zip. What a terrific omen. They never looked back and won by 22 points. All of the pieces meshed. Often, the most important game on a schedule is the first one. It establishes a tempo—a vibe—that sets the trend for the whole year.

It was a good beginning, and even though he wouldn't

enjoy Thanksgiving dinner until the next day, Don Tee-guarden had a real good taste in his mouth.

The schedule that lay ahead was the toughest in the history of the girls team. Unlike those school cafeteria oatmeal cookies in Kodiak that Randall enjoyed so much, these were all tough cookies, well coached with proven talent. Especially Anchorage East, with a guard named Tina LeVigne, strong and explosive, who was the best all-around girls high school basketball player that Don Teeguarden had ever seen.

Those Warriors were still armed with the chip on the shoulder, though, and any team that would win state would have to first make it past his Valley Trash.

Chapter 7

At the beginning of a story titled "The Son of the Wolf," Jack London wrote:

> Man rarely places a proper valuation upon his womankind, at least not until deprived of them. He has no conception of the subtle atmosphere exhaled by the sex feminine, so long as he bathes in it; but let it be withdrawn, and an ever-growing void begins to manifest itself in his existence, and he becomes hungry, in a vague sort of way, for a something so indefinite that he cannot characterize it.

In the Yukon country, the author continued, when the emptiness has become unbearable, the heartiest, bravest of adventurers usually "provisions a poling boat, if it is summer, and if winter, harnesses his dogs and heads for the Southland."

Doesn't that say it all?

Among the earliest American explorers and settlers in the Alaska Territory, the battle of the sexes was over before it ever had a chance to begin. Mankind surrendered unconditionally, and womankind never had to even fire a shot. That was the good news for mankind, too, because so many Alaskan women were well trained in the handling of firearms. You really needed to know how to use those things properly. More people were killed with their own guns than by bear attacks.

Guns are almost a part of the family in normal Last Frontier households, and the .300 Magnum bear rifle is afforded its own chair at the Christmas dinner table.

A third generation Alaskan woman who was going to high school in the Anchorage area in 1982, and once wrote a column for the *Anchorage Daily News* headlined **REAL WOMEN WEAR ANKLE HOLSTERS**, grew up trying to convince herself that existence inside an ice palace was as extreme as outsiders might believe. At the same time, as a little girl she was taught the directive that "the concept of doing the lady-like thing doesn't exist in this world."

The Alaskan woman jump-started jeeps and changed truck tires on icy roadsides. She shoveled snow out of her own driveway, and she cleaned her own fish. She ventured deep into arctic wilderness and set up campsites as routinely as women in the Lower 48 polished their toenails. By 1982, propane tanks were replacing firewood for cooking and heating purposes, a luxury that made many camp ladies feel a little bit spoiled.

The do-it-yourself ethic ran strong. Thanks to their skills at vocational arts, Alaskan women established a solid measure of independence from the men. Alaskan husbands living in towns along the road system were gone a lot, anyway. Men with the good-paying petroleum exploration jobs at drilling sites on the distant North Slope worked a two-week-on, two-week-off system. If nothing work related came up, they were habitually drawn into the allure of the green-and-white wilderness. Any Alaskan woman who was not in school had a job.

Females of the Final Frontier tend to bristle at any suggestion that characterizes them as something of a cross between Ma Kettle and Annie Oakley, the natural offspring of the dance hall queens from the gold rush era. Oh, sure. There was the woman who celebrated her eighty-sixth birthday by standing on her head and reciting the Gettysburg Address. Or the lady in Anchorage who lived in a house surrounded by and hidden behind artificial Christmas trees who sometimes annoyed her neighbors by throwing rocks through their windows. So what? Those types abound in the most elegant of town houses on Park Avenue. Historically, Alaskan women provided a vanguard of a movement for equal rights for women and Native Americans that was unprecedented in any society, anywhere and at anytime on the globe. They never called themselves feminists. They didn't have to because they just . . . were.

Not too many people in the United States know the name Elizabeth Peratrovich, but around the turn of the previous century, her efforts accomplished more for the advancement of Native American rights than all of the congressmen in Washington, D.C., combined. There were dozens more just like Peratrovich. A decade before Amelia Earhart captured the fancy of the nation as a star aviatrix, Marvel Crosson, Alaska's first licensed woman pilot, was setting world altitude records before dying in a crash in 1929.

It was a woman living in Wasilla, Dorothy Page, who first presented the idea of the modern Iditarod dogsled race in 1967, thinking an event like that would be a wonderfully appropriate side feature of the Wasilla–Knik centennial celebration that she helped plan. Within a couple of short decades, T-shirts appeared statewide bearing the slogan: **ALASKA: WHERE MEN ARE MEN AND WOMEN WIN THE IDITAROD**. That was in homage to first Libby Riddle and then Susan Butcher who prevailed in the most grueling outdoor competitive event on the planet.

Should anybody attempt to identify somebody who would ideally serve as the epitome of the Alaskan woman, they could hardly do any better than Sally Heath, wife of Chuck and mother of Sarah. Sally had been the childhood product of the Lower 48, The Outside. Her family had originally lived in California, then Idaho. That was where Sally, who was Irish by extraction and practiced the Catholic faith, met Chuck. Both were students at Columbia Basin Junior College, where Sally was taking courses to become a dental technician. Chuck, who had joined the U.S. Army after his graduation from Sandpoint High School, was a couple of years older and working to obtain the degree that would enable him to teach and ultimately coach athletics, and perhaps become the influence on kids that Cotton Barlow, the Knute Rockne of the Sandpoint Bulldogs, had been on him.

Chuck, it seemed to Sally, was a young man equipped with a self-awareness compass that would serve him well for a lifetime. Thus, he was an excellent matrimonial candidate. After they married and Chuck was teaching, he surprised Sally by announcing his intention to relocate to . . . ALASKA! She was surprised but then realized that she shouldn't have been. Sally understood that if Chuck had any vices, it was his total inability to resist the seductive siren song of the great wilderness. And this new teaching opportunity of his was not just up in Alaska, but in Skagway, for crying out loud, a community that would be most conveniently reached via the utilization of a parachute. And there was no easy way out. The one road to civilization, a gravel single-lane passway that wound a hundred miles through tortuous terrain up the Alaskan highway, was usually dangerously impassible in the winter months. Mostly, travelers arrived on ferries or by airplane, and the Skagway airport limited traffic to one-engine prop jobs. And that small traffic stream was irregular because of weather circumstances.

Many Americans who dream the dream of a downsized and uncomplicated life, insulated from the indignities of the rat race, fantasize about what life might be in a small, tightly knit town that has one of everything. Skagway had one of nothing, other than the school. No medical facilities. No fast food restaurants. No movie theaters. No Catholic churches, for sure. If there had ever been any genuine manifestations of civilization in Skagway, those intrepid mineral prospectors had taken those with them when they abandoned the area as the gold nuggets were being depleted.

With the cascade of gold prospectors who came streaming into Alaska in 1896, Skagway was the staging area for their adventures in the Klondike. In two years it grew to become the largest town in the state, albeit one ruled by lawlessness. A place that was described by an ice-hardened Northwest Canadian Mountie as "just a little better than living in hell," Skagway was an anarchy of mayhem, booze, prostitution, gambling, lynching, and thievery. When Sally and her two daughters, Heather (age four) and Sarah (age two), and another en route, arrived with Chuck in Skagway, those perpetrators of the gold rush stampede were all gone, but they had left their town behind intact. The street was lined with a well-aged and largely unlovely lineup of stark two-story frame structures that gave the town the appearance of a set for an old Hollywood Western movie. Heckuva place to rear three little kids.

But Sally reasoned right away that God had placed her there for a special purpose, and like Chuck, Sally could feel a certain magic in the air. She was suddenly living in a land that was surrounded by waterfalls and glaciers, tucked in around the royal blue lakes that formed the headwaters of the great Yukon River. If anything, Sally became more enamored with the concept of Alaska than her husband. Life amid the isolated cold and darkness would not present a test of faith, but rather a restoration of it. Right away, Sally was determined to ignore all hardships.

If there was a single trait that appeared common to the females of the region—both native born and adopted—it seems to have been that many were born with highly developed coping systems because if they were married, there was a good chance that their spouses—the significant others or whatever the identity of the partners for life—would drink too much. Fishing, and not the environment, was the main reason. People who fished drank twice as much as those engaged in other forms of outdoor activity. Gods knows, if anybody loved to fish, it was Chuck Heath, but while he would enjoy the occasional cold beer, he was one of those unique Alaskans who knew when to say when.

There was a saying in Alaska that when the sunshine began to vanish in October, then the good news was that happy hour was starting and that it lasted nearly six months. The tie-in of alcohol as a cold-weather disease was regarded by some as a myth. They drank even more in the summer months, when the tourists were assisting the local economy, or so the story went.

What was not a myth was the impact of alcohol on the Native American population. Certain hard-hearted Anglos would be quick to repeat the adage that went: "Give an Indian two drinks, and all of a sudden it's, 'I fight you, white man.'" The indigenous peoples, however, point out that white folks have been pouring down booze since the dawn of creation. The Indians have only been exposed for a couple of hundred years. The Aleuts had never heard of the stuff until some Dutch explorers sailed in kegs of rum, and then Russian trappers in the late 1700s came into villages swapping vodka for pelts.

People in the rehab industry don't like to acknowledge this, but sometimes a dipsomaniacal bender brought out the gentle side of a man that, like his pistol, he so often attempted to conceal. Conventionally, in the Mat-Su Valley, when a person had threatened a spouse with a gun, the police report would show that the gun was not even loaded. In 1982, men were scarcer than jobs in Alaska, but the women refused to lower their standards, and the result was an occasional statewide epidemic of sexual frustration.

The place presented demands that stifled some basically deep-rooted feminine instincts. By 1982 the fashion and cosmetic industries had patterned the newest version of the American woman, the one who would rather look beautiful than be beautiful. Well, how could a woman do either when she could only go outdoors while dressed in what might as well have been a space suit. Also, most girls thought that they did not look very sexy in a ski mask.

Any womanly desires to live in a dream home had to have been abandoned at once. Pretty cottage. Two-story colonial. California mid-century modern. Or any other motif of residential housing that most Americans liked to buy.

Brick structures were practically unseen in the Anchorage and Mat-Su areas, for the simple reason that brick was hard to import. But the timber resources were boundless, so most people lived in wood-frame houses that were box-like and somber. Fabricated wallboard and aluminum siding were broadly seen throughout the commercial sectors, compacted into little strip shopping centers. They were literally slapped together, and poorly wired, so electrical fires were not uncommon. Construction standards were relaxed and mostly unenforced. Nobody was surprised to hear stories of Anchorage homeowners whose back porches fell off in big storms.

Interior design specialists were challenged to plan color schemes and to implement the principles of feng shui that could have offset the ever-present heads of large, dead animals and Indian masks that adorned every wall space. Culinary artists were out of luck as well. They might have been tempted to prepare an occasional moose soufflé, or a halibut cheesecake, but home-menu features such as those fell flat. Families expected Kraft macaroni and cheese at mealtime, and plenty of it. The ultimate restaurant experience could be found in the town of Sitka, the state capital when Russia ruled Alaska. The place served a stack of pancakes a foot high, topped with whipped cream. Anybody who could consume the whole stack in five minutes ate it for free.

So there were no stunning photographic images appearing on the slick pages of *Vogue* or *Gourmet* or *Better Homes and Gardens* that even remotely pertained to the tastes of the Alaskan woman.

With the dawning of the Eighties, young Americans had begun to embark on an era founded on the prosperity ethic. The term "yuppie" was appearing in the American dialect for the first time. Madonna had become not only an entertainment superstar but indeed an American icon,

As a senior at Wasilla High School, Sarah Heath stood out as a scholar-athlete who excelled in track and basketball while maintaining a 3.7 grade point average.

(Courtesy: Mat-Su Valley Frontiersman)

The Heath family was well represented on the Wasilla High student council. Sarah appears in the back row (*fifth from left*) while her younger sister, Molly, is pictured in the front row (*fourth from left*).

(*Courtesy: The Chieftain*)

Bear attacks local pastor, bear loses

EARLIER BEAR—Pastor Dick Marsh poses with another Kodiak brown bear bagged earlier.

Scott Anderson

It was a clear Saturday on Afognak Island, temperatures just above freezing, as Dick Marsh walked along a ridge in a narrow stand of timber, hoping to drive a deer into the open where he would be able to get a shot.

As he walked, Marsh - the pastor of Pioneer Peak Baptist Church in Butte - could hear the crunch of snow against his boots with each step. About 100 yards from the end of the ridge, Marsh peeled to the right because the route was easier and it was closer to the car where Anderson was leaning on the hood, eating a sandwich.

About 50 yards down the 35-degree slope, Marsh heard a sound "just like a steam engine" and woofing all the while.

"Naturally, he turned to see what was making the noise - a large brown bear. "The bear was to me in less than two seconds. At 10 feet, I screamed."

In the process, he tripped and somersaulted backwards over a log about eight inches in diameter, then came up on his knees with both hands on his lever-action .243-caliber Sako Finnwolf, a finger on the trigger and the gun pointed right at the sow, standing about five feet away on all fours.

Marsh shot from the hip.

After the first shot, the aged bear turned and ran back up the hill. He had hit it dead center in the chest and at 40 feet the sow stopped, looked back, and turned broadside as if to come back, giving Marsh the chance to place his second shot. The bear was dead when it hit the ground. As it rolled back down the hill, Marsh had to jump out of the way. It rolled 50 yards beyond where he was standing.

Later examining the area where the attack occurred, the hunters found the bear had been laying on a deer it had killed just over the end of the ridge and out of Marsh's sight.

Back at the car, 150 yards away, Anderson heard the commotion and immediately recognized what was happening. As soon as he heard the attack start, he checked to see which of two guns Marsh had with him. Seeing that Marsh had the .243, he started praying.

Anderson, a deacon at Berean Baptist Church in Kodiak, which March pastored before coming to the Butte church, later told Marsh there were two seconds between shots.

Marsh's bear squared 9 feet 2 inches. Measured from its nose to the base of its tail, it was 9 feet 4 inches long. From front claw to front claw, it measured exactly 9 feet. The sow had ivory white claws and its teeth were worn to the gums - signs of old age according to information given Marsh by the Alaska Department of Fish and Game.

Elk hunting was Marsh's primary hunting primary goal during the Thanksgiving - time hunt, with deer hunting being incidental. But because he had the foresight to take along a brown bear tag, as well, he will keep the hide.

Marsh didn't bag an elk, but he did get his limit of five deer - and an experience that will last him a lifetime.

He surely wouldn't have thought of it at the time, but an appropriate prayer for Marsh when facing the animal may have been a few lines of a tune called "The Preacher and the Bear":

Oh Lord, you delivered Daniel from the lion's den,
You delivered Jonah from the belly of the whale and then,
The Hebrew children from the fiery earth, so the Good Book do declare,
But Lord, Lord if you can't help me for goodness sake don't you help that bear!

The adventurous side of life in Alaska was illustrated by Dick Marsh, a minister in the town of Butte in the Mat-Su Valley. Marsh posed with the gigantic Kodiak brown bear that he shot after the animal tried to eat him.

(*Courtesy: Mat-Su Valley Frontiersman*)

Sarah Heath looks ready to attend the prom in her senior portrait at Wasilla High.

(Courtesy: The Chieftain)

Todd Palin won the hearts of practically every girl at Wasilla High when he transferred to the school for his senior year.

(Courtesy: The Chieftain)

Always aggressive, Sarah Heath fought for a loose ball during the Warriors' 1981–1982 season.

(Courtesy: Mat-Su Valley Frontiersman)

The Warriors' point guard, Sarah Heath, found herself outnumbered three-to-one in frenzied competition.

(Courtesy: Mat-Su Valley Frontiersman)

In basketball's ultimate celebration tradition, Sarah Heath clipped down the net after Wasilla won its regional tournament.

(Courtesy: Mat-Su Valley Frontiersman)

Sarah Heath (*left*) and her Warrior teammates demonstrated the "thrill of victory" after advancing to the girls basketball state tournament in 1982.

(Courtesy: Mat-Su Valley Frontiersman)

Coach Don Teeguarden displayed the trophy after his Warriors beat Robert Service High in the Alaska state championship game, culminating Wasilla's Cinderella season.

(Courtesy: Mat-Su Valley Frontiersman)

RIGHT ➤ The assistant coach of the Wasilla team, Cordell Randall, exchanged happy memories with his point guard, Sarah Palin, at the reunion.

(Courtesy: Cordell Randall)

As the governor of Alaska, Sarah Palin was reunited with Coach Teeguarden at the twenty-fifth anniversary reunion of the championship team that was held in Anchorage in March 2007.

(Courtesy: Cordell Randall)

The game ball from Wasilla's first state championship serves as the centerpiece of the trophy case at the high school.

(Courtesy: Mat-Su Valley Frontiersman)

with her characterization of the self-styled Material Girl. The residue of counterculture days that were associated with the late Sixties had vanished and, with it, the popularity of hard-line feminism. That Virginia Slims ad campaign with the slogan "You've Come a Long Way, Baby" had been displaced by the notion that it didn't matter how far "baby" had come unless she was driving a new BMW. Shrinks had learned that it was good for business to assure their troubled female patients that, "You've spent your entire life trying to make other people happy, and now it's time to start living life for *YOU!*"

So as the year 1981 sped to a close, the gap that separated the young women of Alaska from their Lower 48 generation was growing even more distinctive. The blonde starlets of Hollywood never appeared in film plots that involved the habitual use of duct tape or in sex scenes in which intimacies were terminated by swarms of bomber-sized winged insects.

The girls of the 1981–1982 Wasilla Warriors shared one common identity with the players who would confront them on their basketball schedule. They were stuck in a vacuum that existed between two societal eras. The age of innocence—that was long gone, and everybody knew it— and the techno-era that had barely begun to emerge.

Consider this. Heyde Kohring and Jackie Conn and Wanda Strutko and Karen Bush and Sarah Heath were teenage girls who did not obsess on the latest postings on Facebook; they did not carry iPads; they did not share text messages; and they didn't tweet. They did not communicate via e-mail, because the Internet was something that lingered vaguely beyond the horizon. It was not uncommon to see kids pass notes back and forth in a classroom. Social interaction took place via landline, and that had been enhanced in recent years by the introduction of the telephone answering machine.

Google was the last name of some hillbilly character in an old-time newspaper comic strip. By 1982 certain technology-savvy teenagers were forwarding homework assignments to each other on a device known as a fax machine. Also, the more up-to-date and progressive families were equipping their homes with an electronic marvel known as a VCR that enabled them to rent the movies of their choice, not just the ones suitable for TV. The selections, however, like the video rental outlets themselves, were still limited.

The young women of the Alaska of 1982 were existing in a lifestyle more akin to the days of the gold rush than to the twentieth century. Within the vast majority, the only body part that was pierced was the earlobe, and tattoos remained, on the whole, as a fixation of sailors and jailbirds. From the standpoint of pop culture, those were the Dark Ages. The concept of a young person appearing on *American*

Idol and screaming their guts out while the nation applauded was unheard of.

When the kids got bored, they could always go and hang out at the mall. Well, not in Alaska, the most mall-proof location in the entire modern Western world. Alaskans who ventured out of the state, down among the wilds of the uncharted waters in the Lower 48, which to native Alaskans was mentioned merely as The Outside, came back home telling tales of the enthralling new retail innovation of the superstore—Walmart and Target.

Normal leisure-time opportunities, by American standards, were not only limited but almost entirely restricted to handheld Pac-Man games. Alaskan teenagers had but two opportunities to get their kicks—one being engaging in risky behavior, such as sex, booze, and dope—or they could play sports. Happily, many kids turned to the latter choice. Sports offered a lot—a terrific outlet to offset the inherent frustration of the wintertime months of isolation, and better yet, the opportunity to travel.

The act of battling through the elements to play at locations scattered among the Kenai Peninsula, and even to venture into the distant reaches of the Aleutian Island chain, was exciting and eye-opening. The Wasilla girls looked forward to bus rides down to Anchorage with its big city attitude, and more than that, visits to a town like Saldotna or Seward or Kodiak, where aboriginal cultures still reigned.

They came home bruised from keen competition and fulfilled by the idea that Wasilla offered one or two amenities that seemed absolutely luxurious when compared to the settings in those off-the-road towns.

In-state college mostly meant living in Anchorage or Fairbanks. Going off to school almost anyplace was tantamount to freshman-aged kids venturing away to study abroad. They wouldn't be home for Thanksgiving for sure, and probably not for Christmas. What lay ahead was bigtime separation. The idea of visiting potential campuses was largely unheard of among Alaskan high schoolers.

Among the kids who had the resources to leave, and who chose to do it, both the departing college students and their parents knew full well that there was a strong likelihood that their children might never come back. That is, if things worked out for the kids, and they overcame the homesickness and adapted to places where the sun shone, where people did not usually wear thermal underclothes or lock their table scraps into bear-proof containers, and where, when it came to matrimonial choices, they knew that MBA candidates were inclined to smell better than commercial fishermen.

At the Ted Stevens International Airport in Anchorage, the farewells exchanged by departing passengers and the people they loved were prolonged and often heartbreaking to watch. People embraced each other tightly, as if never wanting to let go. Tears glistened on the faces of the parents as they watched their children stride toward the gate while the mothers yelled, "Remember! I'm just a phone call away," as the kids disappeared onto the airplanes. Maybe he or she would come back, but like young men going off into combat, the person who came back would not be same one who had left.

The point of conflict among almost all Alaskan high school seniors came down to one question: to stay or go. Kids selecting the latter option were inclined to have a high quotient of curiosity and personal ambition.

On the Wasilla Warriors, at least one girl had made up her mind. Sarah Heath's exposure to The Outside had been her trip to the sports camp in Texas. In that situation, the concept of change was regulated by a controlled environment. The kids actually resided in the home of the family that ran the camp, located in what for Texas amounted to a rural setting.

But this trip had served to heighten Sarah's longing to experience the different and the new.

Now she wanted to embark on something new. Frequently, kids with Mat-Su Valley origins, if they chose to abandon Alaska and their families to seek higher learning, would venture no farther than the Pacific Northwest or Montana or Idaho, where climate and wildlife extremes were not all that un-Alaska-like. Shortly after Thanksgiving,

Sarah received, via U.S. mail, a notice that her application to study at the University of Hawaii had been accepted.

No two states represented by stars on the U.S. flag could bring a more topographical and cultural 180 than the contrasts presented by the Last Frontier and the Aloha State. But Sarah, despite the almost flamboyant nature of her college selection, remained undaunted. Her airport good-byes would not be etched in deep sadness, because the Heaths knew that no matter what she might experience in her excursion into The Outside, unlike so many others, she would be coming back, her soul intact, because Alaska was in her blood, and that would never go away.

Chapter 8

M_inus 4._

On the morning of Pearl Harbor Day 1981, the mercury in Wasilla dipped below the zero reading for the first time, signaling that the Alaskan winter had finally arrived. Most of the kids at Wasilla High arrived through the parking lot entrance that was situated at the back side of the building, and as they walked past the office en route to their classrooms to begin the day, they noticed a Christmas tree had been put up and decorated by a couple of staff members. It was a midsized spruce, and it contributed an element of cheer to the otherwise gloomy elements.

On average, about 130 inches of snow, not counting ice and sleet, come down upon Wasilla each year, and the forecast indicated that about 4.5 of those inches would appear before the end of the school day. Persons hired to predict the Alaskan weather during the dark months had one of the easiest jobs on the planet. Call for 1 to 10 inches, and you were seldom wrong.

The hallways were not quite as crowded as they had been during the first week of school, because approximately fifty students were no longer enrolled. That was the customary attrition rate at Wasilla High, a place that was securing a reputation as a "dropout factory." That label was unfair to the school and kids because of the transient nature of the population that had been invading the Mat-Su Valley. Some families had arrived in Wasilla seeking jobs and new lives and new beginnings, but they had not found whatever it was they had been looking for and moved on. A few others had been summertime tourist visitors who had become enchanted by the surroundings and stayed. Then Old Man Winter backhanded them across the mouth, and so they'd hightailed it. So, as the Northern Lights arrived for their seasonal appearance that sometimes set the sky ablaze, barely more than four hundred teenagers were attending classes at Wasilla High.

The police were preparing for their busiest time of year. The holiday season, which can be a lonely and depressing time for many Americans was a real doozie and test of faith, for many residing in rural Alaska, and Wasilla, while experiencing the first stages of a prolonged growth spurt, still qualified as a non-urban venue.

The first week in December, it seemed only fitting that the Wasilla newspaper had selected Art Potts as its Citizen of the Week. Potts was an alcohol and drug counselor with the Mat-Su Valley Council on Alcohol. A typical Alaskan, Potts, when he wasn't working, stayed busy exercising his seventeen sled dogs. He said his family was planning to add two horses and some goats to its menagerie of geese and chinchillas. Potts would be a busy, busy man in the coming weeks, because alcohol consumption, among those who used it, would amplify.

In the state capital in Juneau, a publicity-seeking legislator had presented a "novel solution" to the problems that arose from people who misbehaved while under the influence. Representative Frank Ferguson suggested in a bill he introduced that every Alaskan over the age of twenty-one should be issued a drinking license. The politician said this would target "those who are negligent or show habitual disregard for the safety of others. People who abuse their drinking privileges could lose their license." At the same time, there was talk that a bill might be introduced in the state assembly to completely decriminalize the use and possession of marijuana.

Dope smokers contended that weed was a natural antidote for the chronic depression that descended with the wintertime darkness. Some even went so far as to suggest that marijuana was rich in Vitamin D and thus would help many Alaskans to overcome the deficiency caused by the absence of sunshine. However, a letter to the editor appeared in a major newspaper that was written and signed by a girl who said that, while attending high school, she "stayed as high as I could as much as I could" and in the aftermath was convinced that it was not a condition beneficial to the growth and development of an inquiring mind.

Fortunately, Don Teeguarden and his basketball girls were well insulated from the societal concerns that confronted so many of God's frozen people. The coach knew that in days to come, the hardworking Wasilla cops would not be summoned to the homes of any of his girls, unless there was a moose attack. The team was two games into the season and whatever feelings of optimism that the coach had fostered prior to the season for this largely inexperienced group were showing certain signs of coming into fruition.

Ed Frandsen, the high school principal who had hired Teeguarden and who was an old ex-coach himself, stopped by the coach's office to inquire whether the time had come to finalize travel plans for the state tournament—still three months away. Teeguarden realized that his principal wasn't entirely kidding.

"If we go, book a room for Jerry Yates," Teeguarden told Frandsen. "Whatever good this team accomplishes is because of him."

Jerry Yates, a coach who had grown up watching the

spring-training exhibition games of the old Brooklyn Dodgers, had become something more than just a girls basketball coach at Wasilla Junior High. He was more like the director of the minor league system. That junior high situation had developed into a feeder program that would be the foundation of a high school varsity team that might be securing its reservations at the state tournament on a long-term basis. As an ex-baseball player, Teeguarden reveled in the notion that the Wasilla girls basketball team benefited from what amounted to a good farm system that provided him with court-savvy girls, while at the same time, it eliminated the candidates who would never grow an inch taller than five feet, whose sports skills were more attuned to soccer or bowling.

"The kids all love him," Teeguarden continued, speaking about Jerry Yates. "He works them hard and teaches them good basketball. By the time they get to me, the girls understand what practice is supposed to look like."

This group also seemed to be developing an understanding of what game circumstances should look like as well. After two easy wins in the Wasilla gym, they had ventured on the road for the first time for game number three. This would entail a bus trip to Anchorage for an encounter against Dimond High, a consistently tough outfit, and the Dimond gym was always tough on the visitors.

As the Wasilla Warriors ran onto the court, the gym was rocking to the Dimond fight song:

Best in the land
The mighty Lynx of Dimond Hi
Throughout the league
Our rivals hear our battle cry
Fight! Fight! Fight!

This was the setting in which the Warriors would always thrive. The girls were wearing the invisible but ever present chip on their shoulders, playing in the city lights for the pride of the Valley Trash.

The Lynx, looking sporty and almost professional in their maroon-and-gold basketball uniforms, would never have a chance. Wanda Strutko and Heyde Kohring were too tall, too good for the city girls to handle. More gratifying to Teeguarden was the play of his backcourt, Karen Bush and Sarah Heath. They were quickly adapting to the role they would portray as the season continued—and that was acting as the support base for the tall girls working inside the paint. Teeguarden was also pleased by the fact that the Warriors were benefiting from a strong bench. Michelle Carney, who had been a volleyball star, was five eleven and versatile enough to take over for any of the Big Three—Kohring, Strutko, and Conn—and she had made a habit of scoring a basket just moments after being inserted into the game. Michelle would have been a starter for almost any other girls team in Alaska.

Katie Port, a junior with grit, provided excellent off-the-bench support to the backcourt. Teeguarden could rely on Katie to the handle the ball efficiently, not turn it over, and she played hyperactive defense.

The key element to what the Warriors had working was selflessness, which was a commodity that no coach could teach. That had to come from within, and for many, in a sport as competitive as basketball, the notion of self-sacrifice, when the box score was involved, worked against a player's natural instincts.

At the end of the game, the scoreboard read: Dimond Lynx 29–Visitor 58.

Kohring and Strutko had combined for 20 points and 28 rebounds.

A sportswriter from the *Anchorage Daily News* approached Teeguarden after the slaughter had ended, seeking triumphant commentary. Teeguarden realized that whatever he said for the purpose of public print might well be tacked onto the bulletin boards in the locker rooms of each of the Anchorage high schools that the Warriors would have to face later in the campaign if their ambitions to play in the state finals were going to be fulfilled.

"We did quite a few things better than I had anticipated,"

Teeguarden told the reporter in what might have been the sports page understatement of the month.

Every team in every basketball season will encounter games that serve as turning points, either good or bad. Inwardly, Teeguarden felt ecstatic. Those five words—"better than I had anticipated"—did not merely apply to the game against the Dimond Lynx. In Teeguarden's view, he meant his and the Warriors' mission for the entire season. The team had been working and practicing for over a month prior to the road game at Dimond.

The outcome against the Lynx confirmed something, and any preseason doubts or misgivings about the inexperienced nature of the roster had been eradicated once and for all. This Wasilla team was good. Darn good. Just as good as the group from the season before that came so appallingly close to winning the state championship. Just one game short. The ensemble was anything but a replica of the team that hadn't made it. They were not as fast, but bigger—girls who were "long" on the baseline—and the coach was pleased that his backcourt was consistently providing his post-position players with more touches as the season progressed. Still, Teeguarden knew that "just as good" wouldn't hack it. They would have to be a little bit better, because the Anchorage opposition was going to be better, too.

That was due to the ominous presence of two players. Doreen Augeak at Robert Service High School, an Aleut who had spent most of her life at Barrow on the cusp of the North Pole, was an absolute warhorse, a one-woman show. Her coach, Bob Ferguson, said, "For what Doreen does for this team, she is the most valuable player in the state." As good as Augeak had been, she might still draw second billing when it came to the court skills of the star at Anchorage East, Tina LeVigne. The African American player was a scoring machine, and the keystone of the searing full-court press that the East High Thunderbirds employed throughout every game. Teeguarden had seen the scouting reports on Tina, and they included words like "tough, powerful, explosive, electrifying."

So who was better, Augeak or LeVigne? Take your pick, because either of them was probably good enough to have made first-team all-state any place in the United States. For sure, there were no players on the Wasilla team, including the Big Three, who could come anywhere close to matching the talents of Doreen Augeak or Tina LeVigne, and if the Warriors hoped to stay on the court against either of the Anchorage powerhouses, a full-phase, four-quarter team effort would be an absolute requirement.

Ordinarily, the ease with which the Warriors had dispatched the Lynx—a 29-point win on the road no less—might inspire some apprehensions for a basketball coach. Inflated margins of victory could also bring inflated egos and inflated confidence. Teeguarden didn't feel that would be a concern with this group. Individually and collectively, these girls were too focused, too well-grounded, to contract a sudden case of the big head. After the Dimond stampede, the coach offered simple postgame wisdom to his team. "Just remember our motto," he said. "We Try Harder."

The season moved on, and the Warriors continued to saw the opposition off at the knees.

They beat Saldotna. They beat Valdez. They beat Homer, a team with long-legged blonde girls of Scandinavian extraction. They took another trip down to Anchorage, this time to play West High School, the least formidable of the city teams. The Warriors blitzed the girls from West, 46–31, in a game that did offer some special significance. Those state finals coming in March would be played in the fancy gym at West High School, even though West would not be participating. The beating that the Wasilla girls had strapped on the West girls would have been far worse, but the coach called off his dogs early. Jackie Conn, Wanda Strutko, and Heyde Kohring rested on the bench for most of the second half, while Michelle Carney picked up ample playing team.

The West High coach was adequately impressed and noted afterward, "Those girls from the Mat-Su Valley play a more physical game than what we see in the city."

The Valley Trash had struck again.

As Christmas approached the Warriors were suddenly 7-and-0. A poll of sportswriters from throughout Alaska by then had ranked the Warriors number eight in the state. Teeguarden noted that and told Cordell Randall that he hoped the eight-slot would be as high as Wasilla would get at that early juncture of the campaign. He was carefully cultivating the underdog edge, and an attention-getting top-five ranking might mitigate that.

The next stop on the schedule would be the most demanding to that point of the season. This would be another road trip, and not just down to Anchorage this time. Now it was time to journey down into the Kenai Peninsula, one of those overnight adventures which the girls enjoyed so much—the experience of unrolling the sleeping bags and spending the night on a hardwood gymnasium floor.

The setting in Kenai was about as Alaskan as Alaska can get. The original Kenai school had been established by the Russian Orthodox Church. In 1797 the Peninsula, bounded on one side by the Cook Inlet and by Prince William Sound on the other, had been the site of the Battle of Kenai, the combatants being the Dena'ina Athabascans and the outsider fur traders from the Russian Lebedev Company. The Russians, for the first time in the ancient history of Alaska, were routed by the native people, and the Russians should have seen it coming. About a thousand years earlier, some not-too-distant cousins of the Athabascans, an Aleut tribe, shared the island of Greenland with Viking settlers. Greenland, as it turned out, wasn't big enough for both tribes, unpleasantness occurred and the Vikings wound up as a side dish for the Aleut's blue whale dinner entrées.

In 1838, disease accomplished what the Russian fur traders could not, as a smallpox epidemic wiped out half of the population of the Peninsula. In 1848, a Russian mining engineer, Peter Doroshin, reported a discovery that would eventually alter the makeup of North American folklore. He said he'd found gold in the Kenai River.

Not quite a century and a half later, that same river was attracting prospectors from around the globe, seeking a different kind of treasure. Salmon. During the fishing months, anglers stood literally shoulder-to-shoulder, along the banks of the Kenai River, the Russian River, and dozens of other streams and small lakes that adorned the region like polka dots on a pretty woman's party dress. Just as ardent as the salmon hunters was another hearty band of Kenai outdoor people—the clammers. As soon as the ice began to disappear in late April, along a fifty-mile stretch of the Sterling Highway, beaches began teeming with people wearing hip boots who carried buckets and small shovels. At low tide, they advanced toward the waters, gazing into the wet sand for the dimples that identified the hiding places for the razor clams that offered a culinary delicacy that Alaskan clam-a-holics sought with fervor. Degutting the creatures could lead to clammer burnout, but when they were fresh and clean, dipped in egg, dredged through corn meal, and sautéed in butter, Alaskan razor clams rated as a six-star taste treat.

The area was still rich in its history and traditions when the Wasilla girls arrived for back-to-back games against the Kenai Kardinals. Many of the Kards' players were of the same Athabascan ethnicity as the people who'd slaughtered the Russian fur traders. And they were good. Don Tee-guarden, in fact, regarded the Kenai program as good as any in the state. Basketball, for decades, had held a special appeal to young Native American women, who played the game with a particularly keen flair that employed equal elements of tenacity and grace. Not long after the sport of basketball was even invented in Springfield, Massachusetts, a team of girls from an Indian reservation, Fort Shaw in Montana, captivated the nation with their unique playing skills. They performed wearing floor-length Victorian gowns, took on and defeated all comers, and were a huge hit at the St. Louis World's Fair in 1904.

The tradition of the Fort Shaw team was well represented by the Kardinals of the early 1980s. Kenai's gym was jammed and alive with noise and passion for the arrival of the Wasilla girls. Their newly earned state ranking had not gone unnoticed on the Peninsula. Neither team could establish a pattern of momentum. As the game grew late, Wasilla found itself down for the first time in the season, 34–30. The Kards' defenders, the most tenacious group that the Warriors had encountered, made the prospect of working the ball inside to Strutko and Kohring almost impossible.

For every point they scored, the Warriors had to work and fight like they were planting the flag on Iwo Jima. In the closing minute, Teeguarden's crew clawed its way back. At the end of regulation play, the score was 44–44.

In the overtime, both teams were determined not to lose. Kenai pulled ahead by 2 points with a basket that came off with thirty-five seconds left, and then the always composed Jackie Conn, the girl with the sixth sense on the basketball court, retied the frantic contest with a shot from the corner.

The Kards retaliated with just eight ticks left on the scoreboard clock, and there was not enough time left for any last-second Warrior heroics. For the first time in the season, the Warriors were beaten, 50–48. Afterward, Teeguarden's girls of winter were subdued and spent. Teeguarden felt relieved in a way. The idea of an undefeated season had been completely unrealistic, and that was not part of the team's stated goal. If anything, that loss might have alleviated some pressure that was mounting on the girls. Additionally, the defeat had hardly been the product of a lack of effort, nor had it come at the hands of an inferior team. The Warriors had walked away from the court with their heads held high, and they were actually applauded by some of the ardent basketball-hip fans of the home team Kardinals.

Because of the proximity of the scheduled rematch, there was no real opportunity for wound licking or commiseration. The intensity and pace of the second game was a carbon copy of the previous night's game. The setting served as the epitome of girls basketball in Alaska. This was a community event. It was Saturday night, and the game was the only show in town. The Kenai gym was filled to capacity, and once again the place was rocking with electric excitement, with the action on the court bringing a pressure-packed dynamic that served as a sneak preview of the frenzied atmosphere to come in the state tournament.

In Game 2 of the dramatic Kenai doubleheader, the Kards and Warriors swapped the lead the entire night. With Wasilla trailing by 1 point in the final minute and the Warriors facing the prospect of a long trip home nursing two black eyes, Sarah Heath drew a foul. With the gym seemingly vibrating, she stepped to the foul line. On either side of her, fans crammed together on bleacher seats screamed, "Miss it! Miss it!" On the bench, Teeguarden, feeling a swelling sensation in his throat, chose to gaze at his feet.

Sarah, as was her habit, bounced the ball twice, then

took aim and fired. *Swish.* The game was tied. The cries from the crowd, hoping to rattle the free-throw shooter, grew even louder. The referee handed the ball back to Sarah. Two more bounces, and with no hesitation, she launched the second shot. *Swish* again, and the Warriors went ahead, 66–65. Angie Coyne of the Kards missed a shot at the buzzer, and the building seemed to suddenly deflate.

If the blowout at Dimond High in Anchorage had established a turning point for the Warriors, the two-game shootout at Kenai would serve to be even more significant. For the first time, Wasilla had sampled adversity. With the prospect of another defeat staring down on them like a hunger-crazed black bear, the Warriors refused to back down.

The events at the Kenai school confirmed to Don Teeguarden what he had been suspecting for at least a month. This group of girls was a special outfit, and they were becoming more than a team. It was a sorority in sneakers, five girls who had committed themselves to a union that had become as unique and beautiful and rare as a springtime day on the banks of the Yukon River.

Chapter 9

Christmas 1981 was approaching, and Alaska and many of the people within it were being their usual flamboyant selves.

In Palmer, a ten-year-old boy had nearly been killed by a moose. The creature was doing its stomp act on the boy when a brave passerby risked his own life by staging an intervention. Miraculously, the boy survived, though hospitalized with cracked ribs and deep cuts on the left side of his face. He said he'd never go near a moose again. "No way!"

Meanwhile, an adventurer and musher named Fred Agree was encountering an even more harrowing interchange with the wildlife of the Great North Country. Agree, one of those Alaskans who probably did not eat quiche, had embarked on a solo commune with the wilderness. He'd taken his dogs and his sleds on a trek in the Talkeetna Mountain Range north of Wasilla, as rugged as territory can get, even by Alaskan standards.

When he had not returned, worried coworkers informed the authorities, and a search was put into place. Sometimes these efforts turned out successfully. Experienced mushers like Agree were highly resourceful in times of crisis. They had to be, and their survival instincts were off the charts. Still, as the search began, the Las Vegas oddsmakers had listed the wildlife, elements, and terrain as a 5–2 favorite over Fred Agree.

As the search extended into its second day, a forest ranger riding in a helicopter saw something that appeared to be a light from far below. The 'copter dipped down for a closer look, and sure enough, there was a campfire flickering, deep in the bottom of a ravine. A spotlight detected the musher himself, very much alive. The rescuers attempted to provide the beleaguered man with temporary life support. They dropped a sleeping bag and a sack of sandwiches from the helicopter, but the CARE package snagged in the branch of a tall tree. It just wasn't Fred Agree's day. Within another twelve hours, a ground party climbed into the ravine and completed the harrowing rescue. Fred would live to go mushing again, but his story was one that might compel a lesser man to seek a different hobby.

"I had a run-in with three moose," he explained to the rescue party. "I shot one in self-defense, but my dogs ran away, and then I was stranded in that ravine." The following day, Agree ventured back into the territory and located his lost dogs.

So it was business as usual in Alaska, where one of the first things taught and emphasized to trainees in public law enforcement was that it was not a crime to be mentally ill.

On the last day of school before the Christmas break in Wasilla, the thermometer was struggling to regain the zero barrier but not quite making it. There would be a vacation from the classroom for the basketball players. For the first time, a four-team Christmas tournament was scheduled in the Wasilla gym—much to the elation of many residents of the town. The event was already a sellout.

Don Teeguarden attempted to ignore the cold as he trudged into the school building from the parking lot, but he didn't draw any deep breaths knowing all too well how the cold air seared his lungs. In Alaska, they liked to say that there was no such thing as cold weather—just inappropriate winter attire.

One feature of seasonal apparel that Teeguarden wore to defeat the chill was a hat he'd purchased at an outdoor store. It was plaid, with a bill and earflaps. The coach wore it everywhere except while on the job. He called it his Elmer Fudd hat. Teeguarden's assistant and JV coach, Cordell Randall, was constantly razzing his boss about the headwear and his aversion to the harshness of the cold.

"This is Seattle weather," Randall reminded Teeguarden. "You wouldn't last ten minutes up in Fairbanks."

"Probably not," Teeguarden laughed. "And you wouldn't have lasted ten minutes in Vietnam, either," he reminded his trusty sidekick, whose college tenure in brutal Fairbanks twelve years earlier had been motivated in part by Randall's desire to avoid the military draft.

Morale was high in the basketball program. Teeguarden had a notion that he was experiencing the best years of his life, and he suspected that might be the case for some of his players as well. Competitive girls sports was something new on the grand stage of American sports. The Wasilla girls, like others across the land, were being given the opportunity to be taken seriously as athletes and competitors. In that capacity, the coach envied the girls.

Yet the framework of the competition, at least in Wasilla, had not advanced to the degree that the girls were competing for scholarships. It would, eventually. Teeguarden realized that, and with the shadow of financial aid looming as a factor, basketball wouldn't be as much fun anymore.

That lingered in the future, however, and the coach knew down deep that he was living in what he regarded as a time of innocence that someday would be happy memories, and nothing more, in the harder days that life would most certainly provide.

As the final bell rang at the high school, and most of

the students bolted for exits to climb into the rust buckets that most of them drove to school, happy with the anticipation of the emancipation of the holidays, the basketball team was already in the gym. The girls were keyed up for the Christmas tournament, and the coach sensed a special atmosphere of excitement among the group.

Practices were arduous. All of the drills involved running and more running. Conditioning was the key. Conditioning was essential. Anyone who had never actually played the sport could not fully appreciate the demands of the stamina required to hustle up and down the court, time after time; the sheer exertion involved with hard defensive play. If anybody comprehended the rigors of full-speed-ahead, full-throttle, pedal-to-the-metal basketball, it was Sarah Heath, the veteran distance runner. To Sarah, a basketball game amounted to a cross-country race that was run in wind sprint intervals.

The Wasilla girls had taken a vow that they would never lose a game because they had run out of gas. That was something that happened to the opposition. Toward the end of the first half of the games, and then again at the end of the second halves, during the respite time-outs and free throw opportunities, certain players would lean forward gasping, hands on their knees.

That was a telltale indication that fatigue had taken charge. So the Warriors had been trained in the art of body language. Even if they felt they might be on the verge of collapse, unable to take another step, don't let the team on the other side know it. Keep the posture erect. It was all part of the immense mind game played by determined winners that superseded every statistic in the always misleading fine print of the box score.

About twenty minutes into this pre-holiday practice, something unusual happened inside the Wasilla gym. An entertainer named Carole King had sung a hit song about feeling the earth move under her feet. Now the girls at the basketball workout were experiencing the same situation. The ground beneath the building had suddenly begun to shift, and inside the gym, everyone could feel a swaying movement similar to riding on a ship.

Practice would be temporarily halted due to an earthquake. The girls exchanged troubled glances, but nobody panicked. Throughout the Mat-Su Valley, and the entire state, tremors like that were not at all uncommon. Still, everyone felt a pang of anxiety that didn't go away until the shaking finally subsided.

Avalanches. Bear and moose attacks. Life in Alaska was crammed full of sudden death opportunities. But among Alaskans who were there nearly eighteen years earlier and old enough to remember it, earthquakes topped the charts as the greatest of all the state's vast inventory of life-threatening menaces. Alaska tops the rest of the nation in all sorts of categories, with its ninety-seven-pound king salmon or twenty-nine-pound carrot or its fifty-four-pound zucchini, but the margin by which it leads the Lower 48 in the incidences of earthquakes is so great, it's laughable. Except it's not funny.

On Good Friday, March 27, 1964, at 5:36 p.m., a quake centered in Anchorage lasted four minutes, which was (and still is) the strongest in the history of the northern hemisphere. It registered 9.2 on the Richter scale, and evidence of motion was detected everywhere on earth. Damage throughout the region was monumental, but especially in Anchorage, where immense crevasses were ripped open along the landscape throughout the metro area. The building that would become East High School but at the time was Anchorage High was literally sawed in half, right down the middle, with one portion of the structure suddenly resting thirty feet below where it had previously been.

Inadequately engineered homes and stores that characterized the makeup of the city vanished into rubble. At the Anchorage International Airport, the sixty-foot tower that had not been engineered to withstand an earthquake had collapsed, killing one air traffic controller. Landslides triggered by the quake destroyed much of the western part of town. Some areas of Kodiak, over two hundred miles to the south, were permanently raised as much as thirty feet. Gigantic tsunami tidal waves raged across the Pacific, impacting Hawaii and Japan. For an eerie six minutes, the U.S. armed forces' radar detection system near the Arctic Circle was shut down, and given the convulsions on the seismographs down in the States, the military brass had been alerted to the possibility that a nuclear attack had taken place.

It was the real-life horror show of all time, but miraculously, perhaps because the event had occurred on Good Friday, only 131 Alaskans lost their lives. Yet the aftershocks, the psychological ones, still lingered in the years that ensued. The Big One that everyone persisted in predicting in California had already occurred in Alaska, and everybody realized that if it happened once, it surely would occur again. Tremors like the one that sent the Wasilla gym into a bizarre slow dance during the basketball workout provided a constant reminder of the doomsday yet to come. But since the roof of the gymnasium had not caved in, and the walls had not given way and buried everyone alive, the girls shrugged it off. Over at the Mug-Shot Saloon, the regulars hadn't felt a thing.

After the building ceased to move, Coach Teeguarden sounded his whistle and practice resumed as if nothing had happened. Nobody said anything, but with their nonchalance came the unspoken reality that it took a special kind of guts to exist in Alaska.

The Christmas tournament turned out to be the success that everyone had anticipated. Wasilla thumped a visiting team from Cordova easily in the first game. It could have been said that the Cordova girls made a long yuletide trip for nothing, but that was not the case. Cordova had tournament ambitions of its own, and that was the team's stated goal for the year. Every game was a learning experience. Those girls could reflect on that later in the night when they bedded down on the Wasilla gym floor.

The next night would bring a rematch with the Warriors ever-present natural rivals, the girls from Palmer. For Teeguarden, this would be another opportunity to match wits with Assistant Coach Cordell Randall's old colleague Ralph Sallee, coach of the Moose.

Teeguarden understood all too fully that his counterpart on the other side of the court was aching to beat Wasilla, and he knew Randall's old boss well enough to know that Sallee had been lying awake at night, attempting to improvise a tactic that would enable his girls to spring an upset. He was right. Sallee understood that Wasilla's height advantage would be especially costly during the tip-off jump ball that started all four quarters. In the opener, Wasilla had stunned the Moose with their set play that enabled

Jackie Conn to score a basket just four seconds into the game—a play that set the tone for the regular season, which was now approaching the halfway point. The Palmer coach knew his adversary, Teeguarden, as well as Teeguarden knew him, and he totally understood that Teeguarden, by nature a perfectionist, would have had his girls practice the tip-off play until they could run it with their eyes closed.

Sallee knew that had to be stopped. So, before each tip, as he had instructed, one player illegally placed a foot inside the circle reserved for the two girls jumping for the ball. The official recognized the violation each time and automatically awarded the ball to Wasilla out of bounds. So the Warriors would maintain possession, but at least they would be denied the opportunity to execute the play that always resulted in the quick and sure bucket.

With many Palmer fans occupying the stands, the setting inside the Wasilla gym was loud and borderline raucous—in other words, a perfect setting for high school basketball. Amy Guinn, the Wasilla student who maintained the honor of serving as the Warriors mascot in her feathered headdress and knee-length buckskin boots, exhorted the home crowd while a girl in a moose costume did the same for the Palmer side.

Palmer was ready, but Wasilla was taller and won the game by 11 points, and the tournament trophy that went with it. Conn, Kohring, and Strutko—the Big Three—had been their usual efficient selves and were named to the all-tournament team. Sarah Heath had played her best two games of the season in the mind of the coach, especially on defense, making three steals that led to easy baskets. When the Warriors ran their post-oriented offense, Heath, at point guard, fired laser-like passes that made life a whole lot easier for the all-tourney Big Three working underneath the basket.

At the end of the game, Ralph Sallee seemed cheerful as he offered congratulations to Teeguarden. "You're doing a heckuva job here, Don," Sallee said, "and that team of yours is going a long way." He patted Teeguarden on the back. Teeguarden responded with a weak smile, saying thanks but thinking, *Don't try to con me, Ralph.*

During his days of coaching against rival Palmer, Teeguarden learned that Sallee regarded defeat the same way most people might react to finding a rabid skunk in their living room. "To me, losing is harder to swallow than Aunt Miranda's fruitcake," Sallee had once told him.

So now, why all the smiles? Perhaps because after the season-opening 22-point blowout, Wasilla's Christmastime rematch victory had been a bit harder earned. Losing by 11 this time, Palmer had cut the margin in half. Plus, there had been extended portions of the game in which the Palmer kids had held their own and then some. Teeguarden was all too aware that the Palmer guards seemed to have gotten quicker over a month's time and had located some gaps in the Wasilla defense that had not been there previously.

In all probability, Wasilla and Palmer would meet yet again, in the regional competition, the gauntlet that the team must overcome to achieve the bid to go to the state tournament. With his Moose girls' improved performance against Wasilla in the Christmas tournament, Ralph Sallee had constructed just the right pulpit for the sermon that could convince this team that it was capable of beating Wasilla.

Most certainly, old Ralph would ride with his team on the bus back to Palmer, lie awake at night once again, grinding his teeth, and concocting a recipe for disaster for his Mat-Su Valley archenemy. True enough, Sallee's dream of pitching for the Los Angeles Dodgers had gone away when his arm went dead. But Teeguarden knew in his gut that the next time he faced Ralph Sallee, he'd better be ready for a curveball.

So, during the five-day lull when the team would take a breather to celebrate the birth of the Savior, Teeguarden realized that his team, promising as it was, would need to evolve into something better, and he was prepared to develop strategies to enable that to happen. The coach was certain that the Valley Trash underdogs—with their chip-on-the-shoulder mindset—would be wearing targets on their backs for the second half of the campaign. Wasilla's girls were building a statewide reputation for on-the-court excellence, and opponents could make a name for themselves by knocking off the Warriors.

Chapter 10

Upon the arrival of the Year of Our Lord 1982, the Mat-Su Valley said hello to Cachet Teslin Garrett, first child born in the Mat-Su in the New Year. That designation won a $300 prize for her parents, Jim and Gloria, and that had been a hard-earned check. The baby came a month premature, and the delivery was difficult. "I lost a lot of blood. I felt terrible," the mom told the local paper when asked to comment on the blessed event. The dad, who'd also been born on New Year's Day but not early enough to claim the first baby award, was an Alaska highway patrolman and U.S. Marine and therefore used to the sight of blood, and he described his experience watching the delivery as "emotionally exhausting."

That could only be regarded as a good thing, because Alaska was no place for softies and little Cachet arrived already battle tested—just like the girls of the Wasilla Warriors, who returned to practice ready and eager to meet the demands of the season that lay ahead. Some teams that lurked on the upcoming schedule were tougher by far than most of the outfits the Warriors had dominated in compiling the 13–1 record they boasted at the end of the 1981 calendar year.

While the girls were riding a crest of winning momentum, the Wasilla boys basketball team had been making noise, too. Coach Roger Nelles was telling Teeguarden that he might accomplish a rare championship double at tournament time in March. The boys tournament would precede the girls by one week, and be conducted at Saldotna, down on the Kenai Penisula. Nelles, a native of Washington state who moved to Alaska because of the allure of the outdoor life, was the boys coach, and one of several good hires accomplished during the tenure of principal Ed Frandsen. The principal had become fully devoted to the task of upgrading all the sports, for both girls and boys in Wasilla. The season before Nelles had taken charge, the Wasilla boys team had gone 2–19. The program required a drastic upgrade in all areas, but the most urgent problem had been a lack of talent. "I don't care who the coach is," Nelles had once confided to Teeguarden. "You can't win the Kentucky Derby riding on a donkey." But soon, the talent would arrive.

His key player, Dave Lund, stood six foot eight, and possessed good shooting skills. One of the things Nelles liked about his post player was he wore size seventeen shoes. Nelles was an apostle to the coaching mantra that went,

"In basketball, it's not the size of the player's heart that matters, it's the size of his feet."

Lund would require some help, of course, and Coach Nelles had been elated to get the perfect complement to his tall kid in the form of a newcomer who had moved into the Wasilla district the summer before and tried out for the team.

His name was Todd Palin, who was no taller than five foot ten, but came equipped with wonderful natural athletic skills and long extremities as well. After one practice, Nelles realized that young Todd Palin was, in the parlance of coaches of that era, "a stud hoss." He worked both ends of the court with a blast-furnace intensity and stood out as the rare teenage athlete who required absolutely no motivation from his coach.

This gift basket had arrived on Nelles's doorstep from the Alaskan town of Glennallen, about two hundred miles east of Anchorage. Glennallen rested along the banks of the Copper River, a stream, which in later years would become renowned in gourmet grocery stores throughout the Lower 48 for its succulently scrumptious salmon.

The town was a neighboring community to Valdez and had been the next-to-last stop on the Trans-Alaska Pipeline that had finally become operational in August 1977. During the holiday break that straddled 1981 and 1982, it was reported that the two billionth barrel of oil had arrived at the Valdez depot via the engineering marvel that Wasilla assistant coach Cordell Randall had helped construct.

Todd Palin's father, Jim, had been in charge of the power company in Glennallen and had come to the Mat-Su Valley to serve as general manager of the Matanuska Electric co-op. That made Jim—if not a figure of prominence in the community—certainly one of the best-paid people in Wasilla.

Jim Palin was also a part-time high school basketball referee and had actually been a houseguest of Roger Nelles when he traveled to Wasilla to officiate games. When Palin accepted the job at the co-op, he had considered living in Palmer, not Wasilla. The Wasilla coach knew that Palin's son was a good basketball player, and probably the final piece to the puzzle that might win a championship for him. But Nelles did not attempt to recruit Palin. His attitude had been, "If they want to play for me, fine, and if they don't, that's fine, too."

Todd did not fit the mold of the transient new faces at Wasilla High who so routinely came and promptly disappeared. Todd told his coach that his father, Jim, was an ardent sports fan but that he had probably inherited his own athletic skills from his mother, Blanche. She was one-quarter Yupik, an Alaskan tribe of ancient origins descended from the Eskimo. The word *Yupik* meant "real people," and the tribe was known for, among other things, its artistic flair and the wooden masks its members created that someday would fetch $1 million or more from serious collectors worldwide.

Blanche served as secretary of the Alaska Federation of Natives, an organization built to promote the cultural, economic, and political initiatives of the indigenous peoples. That organization was headquartered in Anchorage, and Blanche commuted to the office several times a week.

Coach Nelles greeted the good player from the good family with open arms, and he was not alone in that regard. Every girl in Wasilla High School seemingly had developed a crush on Todd Palin. A few had been known to paint the letters T-O-D-D on their fingernails. The boy was easy-going and fit in well with the student body at his new school.

About midway through the fall semester, the Wasilla girls who had been idolizing the new kid like he was John Travolta could not help but notice that he had begun walking the hallways engaged in happy and cheerful conversations with one girl, and one girl only.

That was Sarah Heath.

Sarah, the outdoorsy girl and sports enthusiast, for the first time in her young life had developed a romantic interest. In Todd, Sarah told her teammates, she had located a kindred spirit. It seemed to Sarah that the only thing Todd loved more than hunting and fishing was winning ball games.

Plus, he presented a kind of self-possessed maturity that was lacking in so many of the other boys at the high school.

For one thing, Todd, unlike so many of the others, did not show up for classes stoned to the tonsils on that good old Mat-Su Valley homegrown goofy bush. He didn't even get stoned, although the right hip pocket of his jeans bore the unmistakable circular imprint of a can of Copenhagen snuff, and Todd's conversational flow included the frequent employment of words that were not customarily used at Sunday services at the Wasilla Assembly of God.

However, Sarah was worldly enough to understand that Mister Right was not also Mister Perfect, because there was no such creature on earth. In her estimation, Todd was close enough. Also, he was about to obtain his pilot's license. Todd had a decisive and certain grip on his life that exceeded the grasp of most high school senior boys, and he had grown beyond the man-child phase. After finishing high school, Todd had already decided he would advance his vocational skills. Money was important to him, and there was plenty of it readily available to anybody willing to take on the demands of the men who worked in the petroleum exploration field up on the North Slope.

College could come later, if at all. And, what appealed to the Heath girl even more, was Todd's declaration that no matter what, he intended to spend his entire life in Alaska. The Lower 48 might have its certain charms and conveniences, Todd had told Sarah, but what it also had was too many people. What was interesting was the fact that if Todd's father had bought a house in Palmer instead of Wasilla, the future Sarah Palin might have become Sarah Somebody Else.

At the dawn of 1982, the flower of life was blossoming nicely for Sarah Heath. She had her first boyfriend. That was nice. And also, she had finalized plans for what she would do after leaving high school and what she visualized as an exciting career. More than the exotic novelty of attending college in Hawaii, Heath was bubbling with enthusiasm for what she would study.

Television. Whether in front of the camera or working behind it in production, this was an occupational field that absolutely fascinated her. If given her druthers, however, the prospect of becoming a female sportscaster seemed most appealing of all. The field seemed wide open. Women covering sporting events in broadcast journalism were not exactly unknown in 1982. In Sarah Heath's estimation, though, they were simply talking dolls—novelty acts who got their jobs via the asset of high cheekbones, blonde hair, and large circular eyes. Not that there was anything wrong with that. But unlike Sarah, they'd never played the games and basically didn't know squat about sports. Those women wouldn't have known the difference between a 2–1–2 zone and a grand slam.

Sarah knew that she could do better than that, a lot better. Her inspiration, and she kept this private, was a strange source: Howard Cosell. The most abrasively big-mouthed and annoyingly boorish person who ever appeared on a television screen, he was a personality who could not have been more un-Alaskan, a lawyer desperately in love with the sound of his own opinion. He was a man who fascinated Sarah Heath.

As long as Sarah could remember, Howard Cosell had been an integral part of her life. That was because since she was seven years old her father, Chuck Heath, had invited Howard Cosell into his home every Monday night of the autumn . . . except that in Alaska, ABC's *Monday Night Football* appeared on TV screens in the late afternoons. Chuck Heath was a huge fan of the ways and means of the National Football League, even though his beloved Green Bay Packers had fallen upon the rocky shores of hard times, and during those Monday games, he never missed a play.

As a grade-schooler and beyond, Sarah would sit next to Chuck and absorb his infectious enthusiasm for the action on the television. Beyond the know-it-all braying of Howard Cosell, Sarah was intrigued with the folksy delivery of the other man in the yellow blazer, Cosell's broadcast partner and alter ego, Dandy Don Meredith.

She admired the ease with which the man called "The Dander-oo" could put down the obnoxious Cosell with his country-boy bon mots. To Sarah Heath, this was the highest form of home entertainment. If she fostered any kind of fantasy situation in her life, it would be sharing a broadcast booth with the man sarcastically known as "Humble Howard." By the time she was into her high school senior year, Heath had refined the fantasy into a scenario in which she would join Cosell on a telecast of a basketball game in which Todd Palin was the star participant.

But when the Wasilla Warriors returned to action for the first time in 1982, the star participant had been Sarah Heath herself.

Wasilla had hosted the Saldotna Stars, a team from the Kenai Peninsula and archrival of the Kenai Kards who had handed the Warriors their only loss. Saldotna played tough, but would experience nothing but frustration against the strangling defense presented by the Warriors. The keystone of the Wasilla defensive fortification was Heath, who came up with eight steals and scored a personal-best 12 points as well.

Afterward, when Coach Teeguarden talked to Gary Grove, who covered the games for the Wasilla paper, he didn't mention any of the names of the Warriors' Big Three—Wanda Strutko, Heyde Kohring, or Jackie Conn. "Our sparkplug tonight," Teeguarden said, "was Sarah Heath."

On the ride home from the Saldotna game, Chuck Heath, who freely admitted that he offered some basketball home-schooling advice to his daughter, represented a point of contention that he had been preaching all season. "You did good, Sarah," Chuck said to his daughter, who realized that the next word coming out her father's mouth was going to be "but."

"But," Chuck said, "you could have scored twenty-five points tonight if you'd driven the ball to the basket. The openings were there. You can score easy baskets, or if not, at least draw a foul. All kinds of good things happen when you attack the basket."

Sarah's response was the customary one that she had supplied on several occasions before, when her father, the coach, the super fan, had presented that critique. She simply shook her head and said, "No. That isn't my role. Not on this team."

As usual, Chuck Heath knew that if his daughter was anything, she was decisive. He would have a better chance winning an argument with a ticked-off moose.

Meanwhile, down in the Lower 48, Americans had received a sampling of life in Alaska. A day that became known as Cold Sunday happened on January 23, 1982. An arctic front roared down across the United States, causing record low temperatures just about everywhere. Minus 50 in Minnesota. Minus 30 in Chicago. Minus 23 in Cleveland and Pittsburgh. Minus 5 in Jackson, Mississippi, and Birmingham, Alabama. In Washington, D.C., the Potomac had frozen, halting the ongoing search for the seventy-four people killed when an Air Florida flight had crashed into the Fourteenth Street bridge. Over two hundred Americans died as a result of the cold surge.

In Alaska, people watched the network news and wondered in unison, "What's the big deal?"

Chapter 11

A person familiar with the ways of the Yukon region
pointed out that Alaska "was and still is the most un-
churched state in the union." That was based on raw
statistics. Among actively practicing certified religious congregations, Alaska ranked smack-dab last, per capita, and
since there was not much capita anyway, almost all of the
compelling landscape remained steeple free.

That was based on a commercial historic footnote to
the gold rush. The gush of opportunists brought in a greed-
driven population whose immediate profiteering priorities
did not involve church building. Just as well. At the close
of the nineteenth century, nowhere else in the western hemisphere were the Ten Commandments taking such a beating.
The incidences of violations of the graven image statute,
which clearly addressed gold lust, outnumbered even "Thou
shalt not covet thy neighbor's wife." When it came to religion, at least they weren't hypocritical. Finally, God had

seen enough. He killed quite a few of them and sent the rest home broke.

Few in number, most churches in Alaska were not much to look at, either. Most were housed amid modest, immensely undistinguished commercial structures. The only way to tell a church from an insurance office was the presence of the cross in front of the building. Building supplies were priority one on the agenda of in-state necessities, and in their pragmatism in the arena of survival, stained glass wasn't big on the list. People who belonged to congregations and attended services didn't care how the structure was designed. Just look around at God's architecture. No mortal could match that. It would be a sacrilege to even try.

Two-century-old Russian Orthodox cathedrals, with wooden domes, could be found sprinkled throughout the smaller towns and existed mostly to be photographed by tourists.

Despite all of that, Alaskans maintained an elevated level of true spirituality. Literary scholars pointed out that the cornerstone book of Alaskan-American life, Jack London's *The Call of the Wild*, was written as a religious allegory, equating the travails of the noble husky Buck with the expulsion from paradise that was described in Genesis. It was all there. So close to Heaven that you could hear the pearly gates being clanged shut every midnight. So much grandeur. So much sorrow. So many different ways to die.

A lot of those regulars at the Mug-Shot Saloon in Wasilla or the Salty Dawg Saloon in Homer started to get philosophical about the topics involving the scope of the universe and the nature of its origins as closing time approached. Persons who were steadfast in maintaining a culture of independent living remained prone to keeping their minds open to all suggestions. In the parking lot, after closing time, they would gaze at the sunrise, see the image of the mountainside in the waters of the lake, and announce, "Look at that. It had to come from *somewhere . . .*"

Paul Riley knew where it came from, knew in the depth of his heart for certain, and he was avid to tell the people the good news about that when he arrived in Wasilla in 1951. He was a very young man in a very young town. They would grow up together.

Riley was exploding with the spirit of the Lord when he came to Wasilla. He was from the town of Grapevine in Texas. Even though Grapevine was situated between Dallas and Fort Worth, when pastor-to-be Riley left town, most of it consisted of a nice filling station and a feed store, and most of the traffic was county trucks hauling away the bounty from the nearby gravel pit, the pride and joy of the whole town. Quite a few children in the Grapevine area lived on farms, and Paul was one of them. Summer days were spent hoe in hand, sharing the tall grass with chiggers and locusts, rattlers and copperheads, scorpions, and tarantulas and brown recluse spiders in the North Texas summertime that served as a post-World War II version of a convection oven.

Because the boy knew of no other way of life, Riley never viewed his labors as a hardship. If anything, he drew inspiration from the words of "Blackland Farmer," a country song that was being aired on a radio station in Fort Worth. A portion of the lyrics went:

> *Breakin' up the new ground early in the day*
> *Gonna plant cotton, I'm gonna plant hay*
> ... [and]
> *Lord, I owe it all to you.*

Perhaps the Assembly of God Church took Riley's background into account when its elders bestowed the first assignment of his pastoral career. This faith was an adjunct to the Pentecostal Church, and the home church in Anchorage was eager to advance its word into the primeval woods of the interior. They also knew that the key to the mission was the employment of messengers who were not afraid of, or put off by, rejection.

Paul and his wife—also a Texan—had no idea what to anticipate when they appeared in Wasilla. This would not be an affluent lifestyle. Paul, unlike Jesus, was not a carpenter, but he had at least a journeyman's skills and was handy in the arts and sciences of the building trades. That was all he really needed to establish a foothold in Wasilla during the time of the Korean War—handyman skills and a heart-bursting yearning to serve his Savior.

His subsistence level was borderline poverty. Paul could afford the rental of what amounted to a one-room cabin with exterior plumbing. He altered the interior of the domicile into four living chambers by the ingenious use of cardboard partitions. Paul thought his home offered a cozy little wood fire-burning ambiance, and he felt blessed.

Many spokespersons of the Lord, particularly the ones serving at for-profit chapels in urban venues, would admit to occasions when they questioned their faith. They said those times could be recurring situations that arose in the neighborhood of the Monday after the Easter service— the culmination of a month-long celebration of the resurrection. The sheer emotional exhaustion that came with that could become a catalyst for doubt.

If certain ministers were vulnerable to a lapse of belief in the True Word, that number would never include Paul Riley. He was unwavering in his assurance to one and all that Jesus was the way of all things real and all things good, and there were no ambiguities in the formulation of his message. The Assembly of God delivered a fundamental, strict-interpretation Old Testament manifesto that offered zero tolerance for sin and vice.

Services were held in the Wasilla Civic Center, an unpretentious structure with stale air. The congregation sat on metal folding chairs. In order to thrive, the group needed to survive—which they did. A group of Wasilla families joined, and the church would add one or two each year.

Paul stuck to the Word, never altered his message, and reminded his flock that, in the climatory extremes, the notion of actually staying alive was a one-day-at-a-time proposition. The Wasilla Assembly of God Church, when the Heaths came to the community in the mid-1960s, had evolved into a community within a community, a spiritual support base in which the loss of one family member was a loss to them all. Nobody suffered illness or heartache alone. That was the type of ministry that Paul Riley had working in Wasilla. The home church in Anchorage took notice of this ministry and bought a parcel of lakeside acreage outside town. That would become the site of the Little Beaver Camp, a youth facility.

Sally Heath was looking for an affiliation for her and her children. The Pentecostal belief system, she felt, was a vast departure from the teachings of the Roman Catholic faith of her childhood, but Riley's approach to spreading the meaning of God's teachings met Sally's approval. Paul Riley baptized both Sarah and Heather at a summer revival, submerging them both in the chilly waters of the camp lake at Little Beaver. Riley's elation at the conclusion of the waterlogged celebration of the saved soul stemmed from the satisfaction of a job well done. He felt that he had formally introduced Heather and Sarah to his Savior, Jesus Christ, and the pastor knew that in both cases, these would be relationships that would endure for a lifetime. For Sarah, she would never have a cause or reason to regret her alliance with the Lord as orchestrated by Pastor Riley.

Midway through her senior year at Wasilla High, it occurred to Heath that she was working on behalf of two coaches—Riley, the spiritual coach; and Teeguarden, the basketball coach. Heath was almost amused by the surface differences between the "coaches." Pastor Riley was ardent and emotional when presenting his message, inclined to raise his voice. Coach Teeguarden, on the other hand, habitually presented his teaching in quietly measured tones and was always the living portrait of composure.

In Sarah's estimation, beyond the varieties in operational approaches, the two men shared a visceral sense of decency and were very much the same at heart. Sarah felt that while the day would never arrive when she might disappoint Pastor Riley, she was not so sure about Coach Teeguarden. He was serious in the quest of a basketball championship, and Sarah, at the outset of February, was mature enough to understand that the attainment of a state championship would require more than a sincere affirmation of faith.

Some of the girls on those high-ranked Anchorage teams

were just as convinced that the Lord was on their side as the Wasilla Warriors were sure the Savoir backed them. In six more short weeks, they would find out for sure.

The Warriors were on a roll, though. In home games, they dismantled West Delta, 65–27, and the next night, they hammered Valdez, 65–39. There wasn't much that Teeguarden could say. "What made me happiest about the weekend was they kept discipline and poise throughout the entire game." More and more, the coach was resting his Big Three. After the Valdez breeze, he noted that Strutko and Conn could have scored at least 35 points apiece. In practice the "run-run-run!" motif had been replaced by a stronger emphasis on shooting drills. The Warriors were in shape. Teeguarden was certain about that. Now he was starting to save the legs that he knew would come under considerable duress at tournament time.

Wasilla—at thirteen wins and two losses—was about to embark on the homestretch of the regular season, and many of the games would be rematches, on the road, against teams they had previously beaten. The girls were guardedly excited about their prospects—even more elated with the nature of the upcoming trips to intriguing and oh-so-Alaskan locations. So the girls loaded up their books and school assignments, their bedrolls and their Bibles, and joyously embarked on each week's trip as if on a grand tour of some exotic Alaskan seashore borough.

Those girls inhaling life on The Outside, with their fast cars and bronzed surfer-boy sweethearts, seemed so superficial to the Wasilla girls as they rode the ferries down to the gyms inside the Kanai Peninsula hamlets where Lower 48 tourists on cruise ships paid midsized fortunes, the life savings of many, just to spend a few hours marveling at the majesty and charm of the area.

First, the Warriors ventured to the port city of Seward—quaint and historic and named for the man who engineered the transaction that enabled the American purchase of Alaska from the empire of Russia. That happened two years after the secretary of state had been virtually butchered alive in a knife attack at the hand of one of John Wilkes Booth's conspirators on the same night Abraham Lincoln was assassinated. In a state so well versed in the arts of human survival, Seward was a man worthy of the concept.

Survival was not to be for the Seward Blue Jays. Wasilla walked all over them, 74–55. The Warriors had begun to ring up some strong offensive numbers, although surpassing the 70-point barrier was rare in girls basketball in 1982. The next stop on the Wasilla road show happened at the Port of Valdez, the terminus of the great Trans-Alaska Pipeline that was in a half-decade to become tragically notorious when a tanker transporting North Slope crude oil ran aground and caused an ecological cataclysm.

Like the Seward girls, the Valdez Bucs had no answer

to the Wasilla onslaught. The Warriors won, 70–43, and Teeguarden seemed almost apologetic. "The game was closer than the final score showed," he said. "We looked kind of rusty at times."

The finale of the trip was a scheduled Friday–Saturday doubleheader set in Cordova. Here was yet another of the sparkling borough communities in the Delta area tucked against the seaside. It was made up of largely equal proportions of Aleut natives, Filipinos, and Caucasian Americans. The town was situated within the boundaries of the Chugach National Forest, at the base of the Copper River Delta, picturesquely arranged among the elevations that rose from Hillside Harbor. Cordova was blessed with perhaps the most moderate climate in all of Alaska, with the temperature rarely diving beneath 15 degrees. In truth, Cordova more resembled a New England fishing village than a mountain-encircled Alaskan-Arctic enclave.

For most of the century, Cordova claimed the title of "Razor Clam Capital of the World." That ended with the Good Friday earthquake of 1964. The shoreline along Prince William Sound was shoved upward almost six feet in some locations, and thus the clamming industry was destroyed.

The various communities that graced the whole state of Alaska would pride themselves in maintaining separate identities—each had a past and a cultural makeup unique within itself. But they all shared one common characteristic, and that was the large and enthusiastic turnout for weekend high school basketball.

If the Kenai Kardinals who had defeated the Warriors in December were the best team in Alaska outside of Anchorage then the Cordova Wolverines were not far behind. Teeguarden expected tough competition, and he would not have been overwhelmingly surprised if Wasilla lost at least one of the two games at Cordova that completed the road trip. The Friday game was a back-and-forth affair, as the coach had anticipated. In the middle of the third quarter, he ordered the team to go after the Wolverines with a pressing defense, using Karen Bush and Sarah Heath as his backcourt attack dogs. That tactic worked marvelously, and during a five-minute spurt, the Warriors transformed a tight match into a near runaway. Wasilla won easily, 44–28.

The encore wouldn't be as easy. The well-coached Wolverines had been ready for the press in the rematch and were strategically prepared. So Teeguarden reverted back to his faithful Big Three formula. For over a week, his Big Three had been reduced to a Big Two, or at least a Big Two-and-a-half. Wasilla's tallest girl, Heyde Kohring, had been operating at less than full speed with a hurt ankle. For a team that was fine-tuning its timing for the stretch run, the subtraction of Kohring from the mix had altered the chemistry of the team.

Kohring was her usual self for the Saturday night game,

and Teeguarden was pleased with the results as the Warriors took the second game 48–42. "The key was having Heyde in full form for the first time in a while. She's been restricted," the coach said afterward. "We're much improved now."

Teeguarden's feelings of good cheer were interrupted early on Sunday morning, when he and Cordell Randall went to the Cordova gym to round up the girls for the return trip to Wasilla. Inside the gym, the sleeping bags were there, but the girls were gone. They had vanished. Teeguarden and Randall looked at each other with expressions that bordered on shock. This contingent of girls had been as stable and reliable as teenagers could get. Disappearing acts were not part of their makeup.

Both coaches walked rapidly outside, hitting the streets and wondering, without saying so aloud, that maybe something bad had occurred. Kidnapped by pirates, maybe. Or carried off by bears. This was Alaska, where no possibilities were ruled out. Teeguarden was on the verge of telling Randall, "You check at the hospital while I call the cops," when they spotted the girls. The entire team was walking toward them, smiling, with Bibles in hand.

They had arisen early and, as the weather seemed pleasant enough, certainly warmer than what they were used to in Wasilla, the girls had decided to attend an early church service in Cordova.

Jackie Conn looked at Teeguarden and said, "What's the matter, coach? You look a little stressed." The coach could only smile and shake his head. The Lord, as He so often did, was working in mysterious ways.

Chapter 12

The structure that housed the Wasilla Assembly of God Church was completely enshrouded in the white exhaust from the vehicles that brought worshippers to the Sunday services in mid-February, the dog days of winter. Here would be yet another subzero day. The wind was coming in thirty-mile-per-hour gusts. The chill factor had to have been minus something ridiculous, but local meteorologists did not bother to calculate the number. What difference would it make?

Pastor Paul Riley felt that this time of year was when his message was most needed by his congregation. The end of winter was in sight, according to the pages of the calendar. But would the arctic agonies ever cease? To many, the days seemed to limp past like a crippled moose, and in the Mat-Su Valley, the residents felt like people who had served twenty years of a thirty-year prison sentence.

Their faith was being stretched to full capacity, along with their emotions, personal relationships, and their actual sanity. Riley chose that occasion to design a sermon that departed from the hellfire and brimstone manifesto that had been his custom. His words on this Sunday maintained a soothing quality.

"Sometimes, winds blow cold coming down from Siberia, but we never really feel the bite, because of the warmth that is radiated by the love of Jesus Christ," was how he began his sermon. Sarah Heath liked that. En route to church that morning, Sarah had found herself humming the melody from the theme song of the new movie in town, *Chariots of Fire*. The release of that motion picture could not have been timelier for the girls of the Wasilla Warriors. Sarah had been especially moved by the tale of the Scottish runner, the aspiring minister, Eric Liddell, who would willingly sacrifice an Olympic gold medal rather than compete in a qualifying heat scheduled on the Sabbath. Sarah wondered whether she would do the same, under the circumstances. Probably not. Paul Riley's pathway to Heaven was founded on a "plow the straight row" ethic, but he had not preached specifically against playing basketball on Sunday.

Fortunately for Sarah, the issue would never arise. Overall, her life at that point seemed nicely arranged. That week, she had been the topic of a feature article in the Mat-Su *Frontiersman* that portrayed her as a Wasilla High School success story. The story cited Sarah's career 3.7 grade point average, her leadership role on the student council, her steady hand as point guard on the basketball team—"always a good defender, she has begun to assert herself on the offensive end"—and identified her as Todd Palin's steady girlfriend. Sarah's quotes were all directed toward the topic of hoops and the team's mounting ambitions. She and her teammates, Heath said, had been committed to winning a championship as a tribute to Don Teeguarden. "We know he wants to win. A lot of people thought we would not be as good a team this year. We got together and decided to try as hard as possible to win for Coach Teeguarden. We've all been together since junior high, and we've become tighter than other teams."

Teeguarden, before the beginning of the season, had offered the girls a reminder of what *not* to say in the event they were asked to address the media. The message was simple. Don't say anything that might wind up pinned to the bulletin board in an opposing team's locker room. Sarah initially feared that, if she were misquoted, that might happen and put her in the coach's doghouse, but she was happy enough with this outcome. She had not boasted that the team would actually win a championship, though she ardently believed that it would. She had merely said that the Warriors would try, just like every other team in Alaska.

If there was an issue in her existence that provoked any pangs of melancholy, it was the knowledge that her days of playing competitive sports—something that had been a focal point of her childhood and teenage years—would, within weeks, be coming to an end. Athletics had amounted to a big portion of her life, her whole identity, and very soon, that would be over.

Girls playing sports at the collegiate level, because of Title IX enactments, had become a fact of life. But not for Sarah. Certainly, she had not received any letters offering a scholarship in basketball or track. Nor had any of her teammates. Alaskan girls mostly went unscouted, likely because of the ill-founded general notion that the quality of play was inferior to what the larger mainstream programs in the Lower 48 were producing. To the people running college athletics, Alaska was Brand X. Sarah was uncertain what the journey to the University of Hawaii would provide, but she was cautiously hopeful of finding something that would fill the void left by the ending of her competitive career. She could always try to walk on at Hawaii but doubted that she would.

Heath drew solace from the awareness that the next four weeks would bring more challenges than the sum total of her previous athletic experiences combined. The road to state, and what she encountered on it, would shape what would ultimately become some significantly defining memories.

The Wasilla Warriors had been rolling on cruise control. In the top division of Alaska girls basketball, the Wasilla team had risen to the rank of fifth in the state in the most recently listed poll in the Anchorage newspaper. That was too high for Don Teeguarden's liking, not that there was much he could do about it. Wasilla High principal Ed Frandsen encouraged the coach not to fret over losing any potential underdog edge. "I think this is terrific," the principal told the coach. "It's good for morale in the student body, and it's good for the school's role in the whole community. That's the best kind of publicity a school can get. People across the whole state know who we are."

Teeguarden knew that Frandsen had been the man who had hired him to coach the girls, and major successes by the team had the residual effect of making the principal look good. And suddenly, he realized that the principal was probably right. None of his players cared a hoot about the rankings. If they did, at least he'd never heard any of them say a single word about it. And when it came to blood-and-guts time on the court at the state tournament, none of the players on those other teams would be thinking about the "mythical" rankings, either. Those schools in Anchorage they would need to beat were ranked higher than the Warriors, anyway.

In short order, the coach would chide himself for bothering with the matter of the rankings. The point was about to become moot, since the team was about to get the props knocked from underneath it. The regular season was nearly concluded, and the schedule afforded one game that would be Wasilla's most ambitious road trip to date. That involved a journey south of the Kenai Peninsula, all the way out to Kodiak Island. Of the various travel opportunities that made the girls basketball experience at Wasilla so enriching, the Kodiak jaunt was always a highlight.

The archipelago itself was chest deep in history, about seven thousand years' worth. That was how far back traces of the ancient native civilizations had been located. Russian fur trappers arrived during the reign of Czar Peter the Great, and because of those men's efforts, the Alaskan sea otter became nearly extinct. Incessant hostility and bloodshed characterized much of the Aleut–Russian interchange.

At the outset of World War II, the island became transformed into a U.S. military fortress. Due to its strategic positioning off the Aleutian Chain, a Japanese invasion seemed inevitable. The invading enemy troops never came, but the main force of the tsunami triggered by the Alaskan quake of 1964 certainly did. The island was virtually wiped out, and many native villages simply disappeared.

The people of Kodiak, as instinctively resilient as they were fearless, naturally rebuilt. Fishing and tourism made the area robust. Kodiak was a proud place, and the high school's sports teams reflected that. The Kodiak Bears were good at everything. The boys excelled at football and basketball, the girls at basketball and track. In the school hallway, situated in a glass case, was at least one state championship trophy for every sport staged by the ASAA (Alaska School Activities Association). In this case, the girls with the chips on their shoulders had added incentive here as well. It was the Kodiak Bears who had beaten the Warriors in the championship game of state tournament the season before in 1981.

Wasilla's girls disembarked at Kodiak from the flight they had caught at the Anchorage airport, and they felt ready and confident. In the initial stages of the game, everything and everybody clicked for the Warriors' cause. If anything, the Kodiak adventure was shaping up as a replay of the two-game sweep that had been registered at Cordova.

Wasilla forged a 9-point lead in the first half. Then, for no apparent reason other than solid defense on the part of the home-court Bears, the Warriors' offense broke down. Turnovers and bad passes were the sources of the shutdown. Wasilla's shooting touch disappeared. The girls, all five of them, went cold, and then into a deep freeze. The Kodiak Bears put together a run in which they outscored Wasilla 17 points to 3. That was the worst sequence of minutes the Warriors had been forced to swallow at any point of the season.

After three quarters, Kodiak led 33–27. On the road in a place like Kodiak, the chance of a successful comeback seemed as remote as the island itself. The Warriors were not content to call it a night, though, and if Sarah Heath was attempting to create some fond memories of an athletic career that was soon to end, her fourth quarter effort against the Bears would serve nicely until something else came along.

Two steals. Three assists. Six points. Wherever the action on the court took place, Sarah seemed to be in the big middle of it. She sparked a comeback that left the game tied at the end of regulation time. That rally consumed a substantial amount of gut-level energy. After two overtimes, the Warriors, who were primed to fight all night if necessary, came away a bucket short of what would have been the biggest win of the regular season. Kodiak was the winner, 45–44.

After the return trip, the girls had but one practice before facing another difficult road assignment. That involved a ride to Anchorage and an appointment against Bartlett High School that, like Kodiak, was known as the Bears.

Bartlett was state ranked one slot ahead of the Warriors, who had slid to seventh after the setback at Kodiak. Teeguarden knew his team would be in for another highly competitive confrontation. They would drive into Anchorage shorthanded. Karen Bush would miss the game. She had the flu. Jackie Conn would play at half speed, at best, with the slightly sprained knee she had brought back as a memento of the Kodiak game.

Perhaps the Bears sensed they were playing a team that would not be entirely at full strength. Bartlett came after the Warriors with an all-out physical effort that was more than anything Wasilla's girls had seen. Bartlett seemed intent on playing smash-mouth basketball. In truth, the Bears approached something more like Roller Derby than basketball. They held. They pushed. They kicked. They shoved. And the more they threw elbows, the less the game officials seemed inclined to call any fouls. Wanda Strutko was knocked to the court while attempting a short jumper, while the ref swallowed his whistle.

A collection of Warriors fans in the Bartlett gym shouted in protest. They would shout all night. Don Teeguarden never felt that his team was being home-cooked—he could not bring himself to believe that any board-certified game official would intentionally favor a team. And even though he disagreed with many of the calls, or non-calls, Teeguarden went out of his way to conceal his displeasure to the refs, and he never ascribed the loss of a game to questionable officiating. That was bad form, he thought, and the one absolute taboo he threw down on the girls was to never, under any circumstances, bad-mouth a zebra.

Bartlett took the win, 54–49, and the Wasilla fans traveled home exceptionally miffed at the "loosely called" game. So the Warriors had lost two games back-to-back, a first for the 1981–1982 season. Teeguarden was simply happy that his team would leave Anchorage with no additional injuries. On the bus ride to Wasilla along the dark and icy mountain highway, there was no conversational interchange among the girls. But Teeguarden could tell. They were mad. They had gotten knocked around by the city girls and had not thrown enough counterpunches to let the Bartlett players feel as though they had been in a scrap.

There would be little time for recrimination. The Warriors were already a shoo-in for a place in the regional tournament, the gateway to state that was coming up in Palmer. One last significant date remained on the regular season agenda and it was a biggie. The girls would take another bus trip to Anchorage, and this time the foe that awaited them would be the team that had been ranked top in the state all season. Anchorage East, led by all-everything Tina LeVigne, would present the Warriors with a barometric reading as to where they stood in regard to the big picture. The game against the East Thunderbirds was not a final exam, but at that late date in the season, it was a big test of how resilient they really were.

Right away, they discovered that the rave notices issued on behalf of Tina LeVigne were not merely based on hype. Among the nine other players on the court, LeVigne seemed to be playing in a separate world of her own. She drove to the basket for layups with such ease that the Wasilla defenders seemed invisible. When she wasn't driving, LeVigne casually popped in fifteen-foot jump shots. Teeguarden altered his man-to-man approach to allow Heath and Conn, his two best defenders, to double-team LeVigne. Nothing helped. Tina was getting plenty of help from another T-Bird all-stater, Stephanie Begich. The Warriors were battling to overcome two road losses. Those games, at least, had fallen into the "hard fought" category. The appointment with the T-Birds, though, was nothing more or less than a debacle. As for the Warriors, it seemed that the harder they fought, the worse matters became.

Teeguarden could scarcely bring himself to look at the scoreboard as he trudged to the locker room at the half. As soon as he did, he was sorry. East led Wasilla, 30–12. When the teams returned for the final two quarters, Teeguarden turned to Cordell Randall, out of earshot from his players, and said, "This is not good. Not good at all. Here's what's getting ready to happen. While we're trying to play catch up, East is going to be playing stomp-butt."

He was prophetic. At the bitter end, and boy was it bitter, East High had beaten Wasilla by almost 40 points. It had been the worst licking the team had endured since Teeguarden's very first season, when the Warriors won only three games.

There was nothing the coach could tell his team, which was not mad this time, but absolutely shell-shocked. "Let's get the hell outta here," Randall suggested to Teeguarden.

The girls dressed and showered quickly and quietly, and the bus left Anchorage in a hurry, carrying a team whose goals and ambitions were in shambles.

Chuck Heath had driven down from Wasilla to see the game. He was particularly anxious to see how Sarah and company would stack up against Tina LeVigne. Throughout the game, it took every ounce of Chuck's willpower to keep from covering his eyes. What he witnessed had been total and complete disaster. He would not express his genuine feelings to his daughter, but the always-optimistic Chuck Heath had become completely convinced that Sarah and her teammates' dream season was a lost cause.

The girls, plus a couple of coaches, were the only people living in the town of Wasilla who did not feel that way. Still, the senior co-captains, Heath and Conn, asked the coach if they could conduct a players-only meeting. The time had come for some serious soul-searching.

Chapter 13

At last, long last, the month of March arrived in Alaska. Salvation from the oppression of the endless night-time, punctuated only by the feeble half-light that appeared five hours out of every twenty-four, lay just ahead on the horizon.

Here was the beginning of the hope-springs-eternal season and, to celebrate its coming emergence, came an early-March outdoor extravaganza that left the Anchorage–Mat Su Valley area brimming, almost reeling, with excitement. The start of the Iditarod dogsled race was soon at hand. In 1982, an assembly of fifty-four daring entries arrived for one of the most boisterous parties on earth. Mardi Gras in New Orleans? Carnival in Rio de Janeiro? Those were Baptist church potluck dinners compared to the annual Musher's Banquet at the Hilton Hotel in Anchorage.

What this dinner party amounted to was a food-and-beverage orgy at which the contestants in the upcoming ordeal could say "so long" to anything resembling creature comforts in the days to come. The banquet took place annually on the Thursday night that preceded the Saturday morning start of the race, and the beginning of an 1,131-mile journey from Anchorage all the way to Nome on trails that were traced along the perimeters of sudden death, an itinerary that led across barren plains of ice, windswept mountainsides, and desolate tundra.

Basically, the Iditarod race served as the symbolic reenactment that memorialized an episode of history that could only have taken place in the territory of Alaska. In 1925, an epidemic of diphtheria—"white man's disease"—swept through Nome. Native American children bore no immunity to the disease, and the serum that could save their lives had been in short supply and was soon depleted. People in Nome were dying in droves.

The serum was available in faraway Anchorage, but the issue was how to transport the medicine to Nome. Ship access was cut off because the ice packs were too thick. Blizzards grounded all aircraft. So a twenty-pound canister of the serum was taken by rail to Fairbanks, and from there a relay of dogsled teams carried the precious medicine on to Nome and arrived in time to prevent the entire city from being wiped out. A lead sled dog named Balco became a territorial hero.

At the banquet that preceded the Iditarod in 1982, a Canadian musher—Larry "Cowboy" Smith—fortified by ample portions of confidence-stimulating bottled spirits, generated a major controversy. Cowboy not only predicted that he would win the race but, "with cold weather and a good trail," he would complete the trek through ice-clogged hell in ten days. No musher had previously driven a team to Nome in fewer than eleven days, and Cowboy's boastful claim was tinged with the most audacity witnessed in the sports world since the early days of Cassius Clay.

"He's either drunk or crazy—or both," countered a fellow musher. "Nobody can complete the trip in ten days. Nobody." In later years, somebody would. But in 1982, inhumane conditions dictated that the winner would not arrive in Nome in ten days, or eleven, but sixteen. The eventual champion was Rick Swensen, the only five-time winner in the history of the Iditarod. For his efforts, he collected the champion's prize, which amounted to $69,000 and a new truck.

On Saturday morning, a huge throng of fans from throughout Alaska and other portions of the North American continent formed a five-block-long human chute that started at Anchorage's Mulcahy Park. The fifty-four sleds, all pulled across the terrain by sixteen elegant and brave Alaskan huskies that were all wearing special boots to protect their paws from the jagged ice they would have to traverse, surged through, while the spectators offered sky-rattling cheers and ovations. Prior to the big send-off, one of the mushers candidly stated that despite the astonishing hardships that lay ahead, the part of the race he dreaded most was the start. "I just don't like being around people," he said, "and all of that cheering and carrying on makes the dogs fidgety."

With the grand evacuation of the intrepid mushers and their proud canines off and running, a feeling of letdown settled upon Anchorage, which was finally receiving increasing hours of treasured daylight but still frozen solid. But the letdown wouldn't endure too long because next on the civic agenda would be the sporting events that stirred the passions of fans along the Cook Inlet and the Kenai Peninsula and Mat-Su Valley, almost, but not quite, to the extent of the Iditarod celebration.

In two weeks, the boys state basketball tournament would happen in Saldotna, for a change, and in three weeks, Anchorage would go ape once again when the girls arrived in town. That would serve as the ceremonial climax to the season, and no state in the union, perhaps—Indiana notwithstanding—was as engrossed with high school basketball to the extent that Alaska was.

As the tournament weeks approached, Wasilla High was firmly in the grip of hoops mania. With regional tournaments at hand, the Warriors might send not one but both teams down to the big show.

The boys team, with Todd Palin playing hard defense and rebounding with intensity, and no team really able to cope with the inside presence of six-foot-eight Dave Lund, seemed to be reaching its peak at the right point of the season.

Then, in the state tournament, disaster arrived in the form of West High from Anchorage. West was a team that had couple of Aleut native starters who, though tenacious, were smallish. West High formed what amounted to a five-man barricade around Lund in the form of a collapsing zone defense, just like the Wasilla coach, Roger Nelles, had known they would. So it would be up to the perimeter shooters to hit some early buckets and eventually pull the Stars back out into a looser arrangement that would then allow the big kid underneath to employ his size advantage. The West defense was certainly nothing new. Nelles's team had been facing similar alignments all season long and usually prevailed, sometimes against teams that were better than West. The state semifinals were there on the Kenai Penisula, always a tough assignment for Wasilla teams. That had been where the Wasilla girls experienced their first loss back in early December. The crowd, because of the ethnic makeup of the Anchorage team would be predominantly West High fans, but Nelles felt the setting wouldn't be overly hostile and was not concerned about the venue.

However, it became evident from the outset that the basketball gods, on this occasion, might be indifferent to the Wasilla fortunes in the state tournament. Throughout the first half, the Wasilla outside shooters, usually good for at least 50 percent accuracy from the eighteen- to twenty-foot range when given the open looks that West was providing, went as cold as the March night outside the gym. They couldn't hit anything and were getting frustrated. Just as alarmingly, the walled-off Dave Lund was becoming frustrated as well. He picked up his second offensive foul when he shoved a West defender in the back, trying to create a sliver of a breathing passage. Meanwhile, two of West's best players, the Fritz brothers, were deadly from both corners.

Wasilla trailed by 6 points after the first quarter. They narrowed the margin to 3 points in the period but then fell back behind by 8. On the bench, Nelles maintained an upbeat posture while dying a lingering death inside.

Things never really improved. Wasilla would never manage to slice the deficit to fewer than 5 points, and when Lund picked up his fourth foul early in the fourth quarter, Nelles's message during time-outs went from strategy talk to a plea of, "Don't give up."

The horn that signaled the end of the game sounded, and one team celebrated at midcourt, and it wasn't Wasilla. West had beaten the Warriors, 59–52, and five months' worth of hard work, sacrifice, high hopes, and fellowship were shattered on the gym floor. Roger Nelles felt there was no need to present a brave front, because it was over and there was nothing he could do. He sat on a chair next to the Wasilla bench, head in his hands. How could something like a ballgame involving teenage boys—just kids, really—generate such unmitigated grief in a grown man?

He faced the media. "We had some problems," Nelles said simply. "It was tough getting it inside. We knew it would be tough, but we thought we could counter. Our perimeter players could never find the range."

Moments after the game on the Kenai Peninsula had ended, Don Teeguarden received a phone call at his house that confirmed the bad news. He was bummed. His girls team often traveled with the boys—both teams and the cheerleaders—forty-eight kids crammed into the same bus and with both teams experiencing a high success rate, spirits had been high all seasons.

He'd heard reports from Saldotna throughout the evening, and they hadn't been good. Now Teeguarden faced a regional challenge of his own. So how would this impact his girls team, which was still trying to resurrect its confidence levels after the shattering loss to Anchorage East?

What would he say to his team? The answer was simple. He wouldn't say anything. The girls' regional tournament would be played in the gym over at Palmer against a field of opponents that the Warriors had beaten previously. He knew his girls would be mature enough not to allow over-confidence to tip over their canoe. They wanted to go to state—wanted that badly. Too much was at stake to underestimate the foe at this point.

Teeguarden still had an uneasy week. In practice, Hedye Kohring had a sprained ankle and seemed a little bit hobbled, although those situations were all too expected that late in the season. The girls looked keen and ready. That carried over to Game 1 in regional against West Valley. That was supposed to have been a walkover, and it was. Next on the agenda was Palmer, and while Wasilla had been steady all season, the Moose had undergone a performance transplant during the second half of the regular season and had shown substantial improvement. It was the memory of the game against the Palmer Moose that concluded the Christmas tournament, the one in which Wasilla had won by 11 points after winning by 22 earlier in the season, that gnawed at Teeguarden. And the thing he remembered most was the sly grin on the face of Ralph Sallee, coach of the Moose, after that game.

Ralph Sallee was not smiling when the two coaches who were actually old friends, shook hands before the start of the game. Sallee, in Teeguarden's estimation, had an expression on his face that said, "Our side is ready." Tee-guarden watched his Wasilla girls do their pregame warm-up routine, with the customary passing drills and layup lines, rituals that basically accomplished nothing other than to ease tensions and whet appetites for the organized chaos known as a basketball game that would soon commence. He watched the Palmer girls at the other end of the court, too, and what he saw alarmed him. Those girls' eyes were filled with hard determination and, even more ominously, they snapped through their drills with an attitude that screamed of confidence. In the two-and-a-half months since they'd last met, Ralph Sallee had brainwashed those girls into believing the ridiculous proposition that they could whip the Wasilla Warriors.

As the teams returned to the dressing room for the final moments before the start of the contest, Teeguarden resisted the temptation to stand on the bench and shout, "Mayday! Mayday!" Instead, he said, "Five minutes," and walked back outside while the girls involved themselves with their devotional moments.

When the girls returned to the court for the regional semis, the pregame player introductions were more ceremonial than during the regular season. The entire squads from both teams were introduced to the crowd in the gym, while the cheerleaders jumped and bobbed and shook their pom-poms. This did not match the fervor of the atmosphere at state, but there was something special in the air.

Teeguarden recalled that, during his days of coaching against Palmer and Ralph Sallee—when things weren't going well—his friendly adversary used to say, "If you want the same results, keep doing the same old thing." So the Wasilla coach had fully expected that Sallee's team would present a tactical format that differed from what had been seen in the two earlier losses. He wasn't disappointed. The Moose presented an offensive look he hadn't seen from any teams that season. The Moose positioned their center at the top of the key and moved the forwards into a double post configuration. That paid off early, as Palmer snared two offensive rebounds and put them back in for quick baskets.

After two-and-a-half minutes, Teeguarden signaled for a time-out. Not only did his girls seem confused and a little out of sync, they trailed, 8–0. Teeguarden addressed the team and explained the situation in football terms. "They're beating us up at the line of scrimmage," he told his tall girls, Strutko and Kohring. "Go harder to the boards."

Strutko's thought was, "We're losing at the line of scrimmage because we're outnumbered."

When the Warriors returned for play, matters quickly

went from bad to badder to worse. The Palmer Moose were emulating their namesakes. They had the Warriors on the ground and were, by God, intent on stomping them to death.

With two minutes on the first-half clock, Palmer had taken a lead that expanded to 14 points. The team was re-enacting the nightmare at Anchorage East. Would it ever awaken? The difference was that against East, the Warriors had confronted a team with superior personnel. They had been supposed to lose, and it wasn't the loss that was surprising, although the margin of defeat certainly had been.

Palmer, on the other hand, was a team that, if Wasilla played it ten times, would win nine games at least.

Teeguarden had been around sports and had seen enough games to understand the anatomy of an upset. That was a three-step process in which the outcome that shocked the fans and made the sportswriters look dumb involved not so much the underdog winning but the over-dog losing it. In Step 1, when a superior team—an overwhelming favorite—found itself behind, players became inclined to overachieve. Every effort became something designed for the highlight film, and the team concept disintegrated.

Step 2 manifested itself when the coach gathered his team, waved his arms like somebody trying to tell a deaf person that his house was on fire, and yelled out such time-honored invectives as, "They're handing your butts to you in a bag because they want it worse than you do, you gutless bunch of (any one of several expletives)!"

Then, in Step 3, out of desperation, the favored team began to panic. A collective voice shouted, "This can't be happening!" and yet the headline in the next day's paper would confirm that it was happening, and it did happen.

While Teeguarden had complete faith in his girls' ability to avoid the overdog syndrome, his plan was to not allow Steps 2 and 3 of the upset anatomy arrangement by attempting to make certain that Step 1 didn't occur. The last thing that Teeguarden wanted to do was issue the command to ramp up the volume on the intensity machine. That would have been an open invitation to each player to go back and attempt to do too much too soon. He had learned early that if you pushed the envelope long enough, you were going to get licked. Teeguarden had also once heard that a daredevil's last words were, "Hey, everybody. Watch this!" Patience would be the cornerstone of any comeback achievement, if there was going to be one.

Down 14 points, Teegaurden called another time-out. His demeanor was not merely calm and low-key, it was nearly serene. That was no easy accomplishment at a time when a person could feel his innards turning upside down.

Men have won Oscars for Best Actor by putting on an act that wasn't as convincing as Teeguarden's in the Palmer gym that night. Meanwhile, his assistant, Cordell Randall, might well have earned a golden statuette for Best Supporting Actor as he picked up on Teeguarden's let's-stay-cool-at-all-costs presentation.

"It's no mystery. We're a little bit behind right now because their shots are falling and ours aren't. The percentages will even out before this is over. Simple as that. Relax, play your game, and at the end of the game, we're going to win." That's what Don Teeguarden said to his team, while his actual cognition told him that, should Wasilla lose, there would be no state tournament and, at that exact moment, his team was a precarious half-step away from going down in a blaze of infamy. Jackie Conn, the maven of "do the smart thing," was one-for-six from the field when the teams returned to finish the half. She thought, "Coach doesn't believe we're in trouble. Well, I'm with him."

Wasilla went to the locker room trailing by 10 at the half, hardly the desirable scenario, but it beat the heck out of 14 and was a manageable deficit. Still, the uphill climb would be a steep one, and in 1982 the 3-point line had yet to come into existence. As they walked off the court, Teeguarden turned to Randall and said, "If we over-strategize, we can really screw this up."

The coach maintained the good cheer demeanor at the

half but instructed his players not to look at the scoreboard for the remainder of the game. "Do what you've been doing all season long, and the scoreboard will take of itself," he said.

When the referee called the team back to the court for the start of the second half, Teeguarden pulled aside his point guard, Sarah Heath. If the Warriors were indeed to stick to their stay-the-course game plan, cool-headed play by the point guard would be essential. Heath knew what the coach would say even before he said it. "Take your time. Don't force anything." Sarah didn't respond but simply nodded. The coach was comforted by the realization that while his team might still lose, they seemed at least to know what they were doing. And it was somehow gratifying to sense that the girls were much cooler, and more quietly confident, than he was.

Heath ran the Wasilla offense with rare precision in the second half. The timing of her passes was immaculate and the tall girls, Wanda Strutko in particular, began to take charge of the ball. Wasilla had cut the margin to 2 points by the end of the third quarter. To start the fourth, Sarah Heath finally took her father Chuck's advice. When she spotted an open alley, Sarah drove to the hoop and dropped in an easy layup to tie the game.

That was the kill shot. The Moose were as good as dead, and their resolve wilted fast. When the buzzer signaled the end of the fourth quarter, Jackie Conn, who'd followed the coach's halftime instruction, looked up at the scoreboard. It read Wasilla 83–Palmer 76. The coach, she believed, was a fortune-teller. True to the no-panic doctrine that rescued the Warriors, all five starters finished in double figures, with Heath kicking in 10.

Gary Grove, the writer from the Mat-Su *Frontiersman* who was working not only for his own paper but also as a correspondent for papers around the state, was eager to get Teeguarden's impressions of the game and this team's classic comeback. He reminded the coach that readers would glance at the final score and think, "So what?" without comprehending the dire nature of what the favored team had encountered and overcome.

Teeguarden employed the advice he had gotten from a speaker at the coaching convention a few years earlier on the topic of how to deal with media people. "Talk to 'em just like you'd talk to a cop when you've been pulled over for running a stop sign after you've maybe had a couple of drinks. Look straight ahead, be polite as hell, answer their questions, tell the truth, and don't say one more word than what's necessary."

So Teeguarden told the reporter something that he had said to the team. "There was a point," he said, "that it occurred to me that we might not be going to win tonight." He felt like adding, "Coming from that far behind builds confidence and character," but that was ridiculous. He thought better of it and limited his comments to a fashion that downplayed his true emotions.

When the team had dressed and was leaving to catch the bus, Teeguarden cornered Jackie Conn, the Countess of Cool.

"Jackie," he said, "you had to know we were in trouble. Did you ever think we were cooked?"

"No, coach, I was never worried." The coach knew that Jackie meant it, too, and felt reassured.

The regional championship game the next night against Cordova was not a wire-to-wire breeze, but it carried the trappings of an anticlimax after the dramatics of the Palmer match. The Warriors fought for every point, played aggressive and relentless defense, and in the end simply refused to allow the Wolverines to put themselves in a position to spring the upset trap. Late in the game, with Cordova in desperation mode, Karen Bush tipped away a Wolverines' press and, in the process of chasing down the loose ball to complete the steal, Sarah Heath rolled her right ankle. Her facial expression didn't register any real discomfort, but she came away limping. The coaches weren't concerned, particularly, because at this stage of the season, every girl on every team that was still standing would be nursing some war wounds.

Wasilla won it, 49–40, and at the end, the team seemed to be more relieved than elated.

Then came the ceremony in which the players climbed the stepladder and one by one, using the trainer's tape scissors, clipped down the net. That was when the gratification kicked in. This group was a Band of Sisters, and they were going back to Anchorage for the greatest show on earth for Alaska's girls basketball.

Chapter 14

In March 1982, when gasoline cost 91 cents a gallon, the Talking Heads, Iron Maiden, and the B-52s ruled the *Billboard* Hot 100 charts, and autopsy reports confirmed that John Belushi had died of an overdose of a concoction known as a "speedball." New faces and new toys were being introduced that would alter the cultural landscape of the United States.

A gap-toothed comic named David Letterman premiered with his late-night talk show on NBC. His first guest was Bill Murray, who performed his own rendition of Olivia Newton-John's "Physical." Simultaneously, or at least that same week, a company known as Commodore Business Machines put a product on the market that would impact lives far more significantly than Letterman's television career. That was the Commodore 64, the first-ever home computer. Also, satellite dishes were beginning to appear on the rooftops of select American households.

At this exact place in time, the dawning of the New

American Information and Technology Age was taking place. But certain things never change, like Christmas and March Madness. The term—"March Madness," not Christmas—was coined in 1939 by H. V. Porter, an official of the Illinois High School Athletic Association (IHSAA). Porter used it again in a poem, "Basketball Ides of March," which he wrote in 1942. Like all great American institutions, it eventually wound up in litigation. The IHSAA sued a small sports television production that snatched the trademark rights. Courts ruled that March Madness was a generic term. CBS's sportscaster Brent Musburger popularized the term for good while doing a play-by-play of the NCAA basketball tournament.

That event reached a national interest pinnacle in 1982, which featured a Final Four collision between John Thompson's Georgetown Hoyas, with sophomore center Patrick Ewing, and Dean Smith's North Carolina Tar Heels, which had a lineup that included Sam Perkins, James Worthy, and a freshman named Michael Jordon. People who believed that the NCAA action provided the ultimate in hoops mania had never been inside an arena to watch the sport Alaska-style, though. By March, the excitement in the stands and on the court was boiling over, and when it came to the issue of Madness, compared to Alaska basketball fans, Charles Manson was sane.

The culmination of the campaign would happen with

the girls state championship tournament, held in 1982 in the big gym of West High School in Anchorage. Here, the combatants had been reduced to the Final Eight— involving two representatives each from the four regions that made up Alaskan interscholastic sports completion. As drawn, those regions brought a whole new dimension to the concept of "gerrymander." Nobel laureate physicists and mathematicians would be daunted to come up with a formula such as the task that confronted the officials of the Alaska School Activities Association, to create a fair and equitable regional arrangement, since the geographic and population realities of the state were so idiosyncratic and far-flung.

The arrangement circa 1982 involved one separate region made up of the Anchorage schools, another region from the southeast corner of the state along the Alexander Archipelago, another northern region that included high schools from an area that encompassed roughly 500,000 square miles, and finally a fourth region (technically Region III) that was divided into North and South Zones. Teams from the Mat-Su Valley and the Valdez-Cordova area, about 350 miles from the Mat-Su Valley, were shoehorned into the North Zone. The South was made up of schools on the Kenai Peninsula and Kodiak Island. If that seemed like an odd, almost screwy setup, and the administrators who designed the blueprint did so with the disclaimer that should anybody think they could do it better, then they were open to suggestions.

If the NCAA tournament was famous for its Sweet Sixteen and Final Four, Alaska's tournament could lay claim to its Great Eight. The honorees for the girls championships in 1982 were as follows. East High School and Robert Service represented the Anchorage Region. Two high schools from Fairbanks, Lathrop and Monroe Catholic, came down from the vast Upper Region. Petersburg and Juneau-Douglas, a high school that would later produce NBA superstar Carlos Boozer, were the finalists from the Southeast Region and, last and in that season seemingly least, the Region III schools, the Kenai Kardinals who had won the South Zone tournament, and the North Zone team, the Wasilla Warriors.

As tournament time approached, that last-mentioned team might as well have referred to itself as the Wasilla Afterthoughts. They were listed as the second seed from their Region III, by virtue of having lost twice to the Kenai Kards during the regular season.

Don Teeguarden, on the Monday before the three-day weekend extravaganza, had driven to Anchorage for a pre-tournament coach's meeting. As a joke, Teeguarden arrived at the session wearing his infamous Elmer Fudd hat.

"What the hell's that?" one of the coaches laughed.

"Oh, I think I am going to do a little bird hunting," Teeguarden said.

"Watch it!" responded Bob Durado, coach of Anchorage East, whose team was known as the Thunderbirds. Durado, of the eight coaches assembled, was the one who could most afford an attitude of levity as his team was the overwhelming favorite to dominate the field of eight.

The tournament brackets were drawn. In the opening round game on Thursday night, the second seed from Region III would play the top seed from Region II. So that meant—guess what?—the Wasilla Warriors, right off, would be tossed into the burning cauldron that was Anchorage East—the team that had humiliated Wasilla by nearly 40 points in its final regular season game. The only good news, if the Warriors chose to look at it that way, was that they were not the only team that had been all but tarred and feathered by the powerhouse girls from East High School.

Prior to the coach's meeting, Teeguarden had glanced through that day's issue of the *Anchorage Daily News*. The paper included a little feature it called "Employee of the Day," and on that occasion, the person being featured was Odell Fox, a janitor. The thing that Mr. Fox liked about his occupation was, he said, "I don't have to worry about the threat of my job being terminated. Even the president in Washington needs janitorizing."

Given his weekend assignment, Teeguarden mused that he might consider trading places with Odell Fox. With East bearing down on the Warriors like a freight train, his prospects seemed grim. Back in Wasilla, around town and at the high school, the Warriors' loyalists seemed grim, in a polite kind of way. Teeguarden was halfway expecting to receive some greeting cards in the mail—cards adorned with flowers—with the inscription: **SORRY ABOUT YOUR LOSS**.

When the Wasilla fans learned the identity of the first-round opponent, the universal reaction had been, "Jeez. What a bummer."

Teeguarden, in truth, felt that his team had a chance against East. This was a sporting event after all. Anything could happen. The factor that gave the coach the most hope, though, was the attitude of the girls. These were kids who had experienced the whipping, and in practice, while not exactly oozing with confidence, Teeguarden could sense that his team was at least not scared of the Thunderbirds. The girls were convinced that the earlier outcome had been an aberration.

After that debacle, Teeguarden had momentarily considered staging a ceremonial ritual burning of the tape of the East game. Fortunately, since that had been the end of the regular season, the girls had no time to dwell on the magnitude of the defeat, since they quickly needed to prepare for and focus on the upcoming regional tournament at Palmer, the door-die entry exam for the state tournament.

Teeguarden felt convinced that the game would be closer in the rematch, because the Warriors would employ a whole new defensive format. In the regular season game, Wasilla had come at East with a man-to-man setup and gotten torched all night. In the encore, the Warriors attempted to slow down the T-Birds with a 2–3 zone setup, which had been their most effective tactic throughout the season. Teeguarden, in fact, would use a man-to-man defense against teams that he guessed his team would face in the postseason, and then use the zone in the rematch for the element of surprise, if nothing else.

After the final Wednesday practice for the Thursday night game in Anchorage, Teeguarden felt his girls looked as sharp and ready as they had all season. There was one concern, though, and he feared it might be a major one. Sarah Heath had sustained what appeared to have been a high ankle sprain in the regional final against Cordova. She would not be at 100 percent playing capacity for the state tournament, perhaps not even 80.

At home, Chuck Heath realized that his daughter was hurt. His notion was that Sarah might be better off sitting out the game, because if she reinjured the ankle, her track season might be in jeopardy. Chuck knew better than to ever suggest that, though, just as he knew he wouldn't articulate the fact that he thought Wasilla's odds against East amounted to the proverbial snowball's chance in hell.

All too soon, Thursday arrived. The sports section of the *Anchorage Daily News* was crammed with articles about the event. The thrust of the ink was the likely event of an all-Anchorage finals—East versus Robert Service.

Bob Ferguson, coach of the Service Cougars, sounded not only hopeful but cocky to the point of audacious. Like Wasilla, Service had been flattened by the T-Birds in a regular season game, but a rematch had produced a closer result. Ferguson noted that his team had won just three games in the 1979–1980 season, and he trumpeted, "Look where we are now. As far as East goes, we have gotten closer and closer, and that gives us a psychological edge. I think they might be scared of us." Here, Ferguson was clearly playing a risky mind game. But why not? What did he have to lose? The coach went on to rave about his star guard, Doreen Augeak, noting her ball-handling skills and "quick scoring ability."

Then Ferguson reiterated a quote from earlier in the season, asserting that, "Given what she provides for us, I think that Doreen is the most valuable player in the state."

Teeguarden had left Wasilla ahead of the team bus, wanting to watch some day games that would precede the evening finale—East against Wasilla. The gym was filling up. Both schools from Fairbanks, Lathrop and Monroe, won and eliminated the entries from the southeast region, Petersburg and Juneau-Douglas. Then Bob Ferguson's Service Cougars lived up to their coach's pre-tournament billing, and knocked off the Kenai Kards, the team that had beaten Wasilla two-out-of-three regular season contests. Maybe Service was every bit as good as the confident coach thought they were. The final score had been Robert Service 54–Kenai 44. Doreen Augeak scored 28 points.

But Teeguarden was more impressed with one of the Fairbanks teams than he was with Service. That was Monroe, the northernmost Catholic high school in the world. The Rams were lightning quick and well coached. As he evaluated the personnel, Teeguarden sensed that Monroe would offer big-time match-up problems against his Warriors—in the long-shot event that the game might ever take place.

Near the end of the Service–Kenai game, the bus from Wasilla arrived at West High School. In the locker room, Teeguarden was, as usual, low-key. The girls knew what had to be done. The conclusion of a satisfying season, a season in which the Wasilla girls had indeed lived up to their potential by winning twenty of twenty-five games, plus a regional championship, was then at hand.

The girls seemed not subdued, but they were quiet. The seniors realized fully that they very well might be about to play the last game of an activity that had been a major source of joy in their lives since they had been in grade school, learning the basics of the sports in the Little Dribblers program. That special cohesive sisterhood that had been crafted under coach Jerry Yates at the junior high school, all of that was about to enter the final chapter. It was as if the 1981–1982 season had blossomed into something beautiful, a journey of fulfillment, and they did not want to see it end.

For Don Teeguarden, there was nothing left to say to the girls, except, "Good luck."

As the girls trotted on the gym floor for their pregame drills, and the Wasilla fans greeted them with a roar, Sarah Heath offered some encouraging words to her coach. The injured ankle, though heavily taped, felt, "Just fine." Sarah assured Teeguarden that she was ready to go. Teeguarden really hoped so, because if the Warriors were to stand a prayer against East, all cylinders would have to be firing the entire night.

If the East T-Birds were afraid of playing Anchorage Service again, as Bob Ferguson had suggested in print, then they certainly were not afraid of the Wasilla Warriors. Wasilla's assistant coach Cordell Randall, was amazed at the attitude and body language of the T-Birds, as they yukked it up in the pregame shootaround, and grinned and waved at friends in the stands.

The fans broke into a spontaneous rendering of their fight song, singing and clapping.

We'll fight and win this game, to bring honor to the name;
Of the loyal Thunderbird, and great East Anchorage High.

Yes, East High—players and fans alike—were cocked and loaded and ready to take off. "They think they're going to chop us into cat food," Randall told Teeguarden, who was not entirely certain whether that was a good thing or not.

While the Wasilla fans were numerous, loud, and supportive, they were outnumbered and outyelled by the legion of T-Birds fans from the big high school across town on Northern Lights Boulevard in Anchorage's Green Belt district. The school, in fact, was situated in one of those parts of Anchorage from which Mount McKinley was visible, and where the moose roamed the neighborhood. East was the most culturally diverse of all the Anchorage schools, and the lineup of their girls basketball team reflected that.

And then the waiting was over.

East controlled the tip, and right away, the Tina LeVigne show was underway.

This African American girl was a basketball natural. With long legs attached to a high, lean waist, LeVigne had the build of a major league baseball pitcher, and she played the game with a special element of fluid grace, like a professional dancer. When William Shakespeare wrote of "the action of the tiger" in *Henry V,* he might just as well have been writing about Tina LeVigne.

From the very start, Tina began the assault, firing twenty-foot rainbows. In high school girls basketball competition, many of the field goals went in after bouncing off the rim or the backboard. But with Tina, time after time, it was nothing but net.

The T-Birds cruised off to a quick lead. But largely, the margin was of, for, and by Tina LeVigne. Wasilla's revolving, sagging zone defense provided a three-player umbrella that separated the T-Birds' post players from the lethal LeVigne.

Unlike during the regular season game, Wassila's offense began to click. This time, they were cracking through East's full-court press, and once the ball advanced past half-court, slivers of daylight were available underneath. Wanda Strutko was scoring from inside. So was Heyde Kohring. Jackie Conn pumped in two baskets from the corner.

Teeguarden was astonished at the pace of the game, which had evolved into a furious, back-and-forth battle. Fighting for their basketball lives, the Warriors had taken their game up to a notch that the coach did not realize they had. The Thunderbirds were equal to the occasion.

They still led after the first quarter, but by then, it had become evident that here in the state tournament, this rematch would be no runaway.

The halftime score of the regular season game—East 30–Wasilla 12—had been seared into Teeguarden's memory. This time, Wasilla's 1-point deficit at the intermission had a considerably better flavor. His halftime message was succinct and to the point. Keep it up. He offered one point of encouragement: "The zone is working pretty good. They (East) don't have a lot of punch underneath this time."

The frantic nature of play continued through the third quarter, and into the fourth. The score began to seesaw, as the Warriors dived and lunged for the vital 50-50 balls like a mother leaping to save her child from the window ledge of a burning building. They generated turnovers. Tina LeVigne, at times, had begun to seem almost human. She missed a few, and when she did, Strutko and Kohring, always snagged the rebound.

Two minutes into the fourth quarter, Teeguarden looked at the scoreboard. His red-clad Warriors were up by 5. But East, rather than abandon their poise in the face of an upset disaster, maintained their cool. If Tina LeVigne was feeling frustration, she didn't play like it. The T-Birds cut the margin to 43–42 with 5:01 to play, and then turned cold.

There, with the gym quaking and the pressure so intense that it seemed the roof might blow off the building,

Wasilla put forth a burst that amounted to the best basketball that Teeguarden would witness during his entire tenure in the Mat-Su Valley. His Warriors reeled off 5 unanswered points, and with ninety seconds to play, Wasilla led the T-Birds, 50–44.

Ferocious and prideful, the T-Birds were not about to concede. Stephanie Begich, East's other all-star player, nailed a baseline jumper with 1:01 left on the clock. Then the T-Birds registered a steal of their own. Naturally, the ball went into the hands of Tina LeVigne, who took the ball inside, for a change, and scored on a driving layup with 16 seconds left, cutting Wasilla's margin to 2 points.

The Warriors beat the press, one final time, and as Wanda Strutko drove toward the T-Birds' basket, it was none other than Tina LeVigne who jumped into her path, attempting to draw a charging call. Both Strutko and LeVigne were shouldering four fouls, a fifth and the game was over for one of them and possibly their teams as well. The collision between the two girls was tremendous. Both fell to the floor, and now the game was in the hands of the official. When the dust settled, and the gym suddenly and almost eerily silent, he issued the verdict. The foul was on Tina Levigne.

Still, the drama would not end. Strutko missed the front end of her 1-and-1, and then the official sounded his whistle again. Jackie Conn had been charged with a foul for reaching. The girls marched back to the other end of the court.

Begich was given a 1-and-1 opportunity to tie the game with one second left. She missed. Game over.

On the T-Birds' bench, a man with a vacant stare attempted to comprehend what had just taken place. "I don't know what happened," was all that East coach Bob Durado could think to say. "I wish I did."

On Friday morning, a headline ran across the top of the first page of the sports section of the *Anchorage Daily News*: **WASILLA GIRLS STUN EAST.**

Yes, they did, and the heart continued to beat on the Warriors' dream season.

Chapter 15

If Sarah Heath had drawn inspiration in 1982 from the Oscar–winning motion picture *Chariots of Fire* and the Scottish runner whose Christian faith surpassed all else, then her father, Chuck, could well have been accused of adopting Sylvester Stallone as a role model of his own.

In the 1976 film *Rocky,* the underdog hero, Rocky Balboa, rose before dawn, chug-a-lugged six raw eggs, and then ran through the streets of South Philly to gain stamina for his upcoming match for the heavyweight title. Heath probably eschewed the eggs, but his training routine that happened most mornings while most of the rest of the community was still asleep, eclipsed what Rocky was doing on the silver screen in terms of sheer masochistic hardship.

Most days, when the winds were favorable, Chuck would rise around 4:30 a.m., dress appropriately for the ordeal, than have his wife Sally drive him all the way to Palmer, from where he would run back to Wasilla, a solitary figure jogging eight miles—almost one third of a marathon—along the road shoulder. That was Heath's conditioning routine for his attempt to run the Boston Marathon. In January, that meant the run would take place in subzero weather. He always ran downwind. Anything else would have been suicidal. Heath always donned a ski mask and also equipped himself with what he called a "crotch rag," a device recommended to him by an elite Alaskan distance runner who recounted a training experience amid bitter arctic conditions in which he'd literally frozen his testicles.

That bit of advice had made an impression on Chuck. He was a tough man, but he had to draw the line somewhere. By the third week of March, running conditions had been growing almost tolerable. Sometimes the temperature would reach as high as 15 degrees, far more agreeable than the subzero nightmare that he had forced himself to withstand earlier in the winter. He was happy with his progress, which was good, because the annual Patriot's Day marathon would occur in only six weeks.

While attempting to master the fine art of distance running, so that he could pass on his knowledge to the cross-country kids he was coaching, Chuck had learned early to let his mind wander into a different place during the grueling practice grind. Think happy and peaceful thoughts and ignore that imposter called pain. Frequently, Chuck would concentrate on the genuinely happy and peaceful reality that for him in Alaska was good. That bold adventure, the gamble—to abandon the Lower 48 for an existence in winters that were as cold and dark as a tomb—had paid off.

That Skagway adventure had been something to remember. Heath told friends that he had liked the primitive setting but moved away after one year to obtain his graduate degree. His actual motivation had been something else. While Sally had never complained, it was Chuck Heath who decided that Skagway, for all of its scenic and historical appeal, was no place to bring up a houseful of well-adjusted children.

Wasilla was different, a family-based culture for sure. The community was healthy and thriving. According to the 1930 census, exactly 51 people called Wasilla home. By 1980, the population of the town had expanded to over 1,500 and, by 1990, it would surpass 4,000. The Heaths had found contentment and security there. Financially, they were well-enough off, with Chuck's teaching and moonlight-coaching income, and Sally's employment as a school secretary. In 1982, the household budget would be further enhanced by $6,000 from the Alaska Permanent Fund (APF).

That arrangement paid an annual dividend to every

citizen of the state as their rightful share of the mineral bounty coming down from the North Slope in the Trans-Alaska Pipeline. For a large percentage of Alaskans, especially in the remote native villages deep in the frozen arctic outback, the APF check went straight to the liquor store. In the Heath family, the money was being set aside in a college fund for the four kids.

On the Friday morning Palmer-to-Wasilla jaunt that was happening on the first day of spring, Heath's mental focus did not involve career, finances, or the Boston Marathon. He was still engrossed in what had happened the night before. The Wasilla Warriors had sprung what might have been, and probably was, the most remarkable upset in the history of Alaskan athletics.

Their 2-point victory over Anchorage East in a game that had literally come down to the final second would have the whole town ablaze with amazement and joy. The outcome of the game had been the biggest boon for Wasilla since the railroad came to town in 1917. After having lost to the state's top-ranked team by nearly 40 points, and then coming back to win the rematch that really mattered, Chuck Heath thought it might make a good plot for a movie some producer could call *The Revenge of the Valley Trash*.

Chuck Heath, of course, had numbered himself among the ranks of the nonbelievers. He had been eager to get Sarah's account of the combat when she returned home late Thursday night, nearly exhausted, with a slight hint of "I told you so" glittering in her eyes.

Mostly, Sarah had limited her account of the night's proceedings to merely comment on what she felt had been the extraordinary sportsmanship demonstrated by the Thunderbird players after the game. "They came over and told us that the best team won," Sarah told her parents, and said that the great Tina LeVigne had shaken her hand and told her that she would be rooting for Wasilla to win the state championship. Then Sarah had iced down her badly swollen ankle and gone to bed. Another tournament test loomed ahead on Friday night, but before that happened, Friday morning was still a school day.

The many Wasillans who had chosen not to drive to Anchorage to watch the state tournament opener against East High School, having dismissed the mission as a lost cause, were wishing they had. Most of the ones who stayed behind had at least been tuned into the tournament pandemonium via the robust account of the cage classic delivered by Curt Menard and Hugh Mathison, the radio voices of the Wasilla Warriors. That duo worked the games for a Wasilla radio station, KABN, fittingly known as "The Cabin," and the tone of their accounts of the games could hardly have been termed as unbiased. Menard was perhaps Wasilla's most prominent dentist, active in local politics and civic affairs, and he had children who played various sports at the high school. Mathison was an administrator with the school district.

The pair worked as a great tandem partnership, with a down-home and informal broadcast chemistry that might have been reminiscent of the days when Dizzy Dean and Pee Wee Reese were doing the Major League Baseball Game of the Week on CBS during the Fifties and earlier Sixties. During those telecasts, Old Diz would be loaded on the sponsor's product, Falstaff beer, by the fifth inning, and would start singing his version of "The Wabash Cannonball" by the seventh.

Menard and Mathison, in their genuine feel-good enthusiasm, didn't require any assistance from "the choicest product of the brewer's art" to bring life to their play-by-play and color their delivery. They were out-and-out and blatant "homers," cheering the Warriors on from start to finish, and chiding the game officials on calls that went against Wasilla. Their game accounts would run the gamut from "Gee whiz!" to "Aw, shucks!"

At the finish, when Menard told his listeners that the victory over East had been "the most exciting game ever, ever seen in the great state of Alaska," nobody in Wasilla had been willing to argue, although some purists might have suggested that Petersburg High's 1939 triumph over the Juneau fire department rivaled it.

As the town woke up on Friday morning, everybody

was rushing to the stores to buy a newspaper account of the huge Wasilla triumph. Since the Mat-Su Valley *Frontiersman* did not publish a Friday edition, readers would have to make due with a game account from the Anchorage paper. *Anchorage Daily News* sportswriter Mike Grady would not let them down. In a vivid account of the contest, this same scribe who had not even mentioned Wasilla in his pre-tournament stories, offered rich praise for the dazzling performance of the Warriors:

Wasilla's Warriors grabbed the limelight of the girls state basketball tournament. The Wasilla girls used a height advantage and an intelligent attack on East's vaunted full court press to produce the upset.

Tina LeVigne was on fire, with an early outburst that would eventually lead to a twenty-six point performance for the night. She put the Warriors in a hole early, and pumped in twelve points from the top of the key in the first quarter alone.

Then Wasilla's top three defenders, Jackie Conn, Sarah Heath and Karen Bush, got tough and made LeVigne work for every point she would score for the remainder of the game. Rather than let LeVigne put the ball on the floor, the trio started to converge. Then it was a steal or two here, a loose ball or three there, and suddenly the Warriors were off to the races.

That was what Don Teeguarden saw as well as he watched the tape of the game in the early morning hours in his coaching office at the high school. He could scarcely believe what he was seeing, and unlike the tape of the regular season game against East, this was not a tape he would be tempted to toss into a blazing fireplace.

The Thunderbirds had not lost through any lack of intensity. Teeguarden did feel that East lacked a certain sharp edge, due to nearly two weeks of inactivity. They had not participated in a regional tournament and had earned a bye into the state tournament because of the team's top-ranked status. So the T-Birds might have been a trifle rusty. If that had been the final determinant in the upset, then so be it. Bob Durado, the East coach, had at least offered no excuses after the game.

Teeguarden had heard talk that the National Basketball Association was considering adding a 3-point basket for long range, and if that happened, the novelty would soon pass down to the college and high school games. As he reviewed the tape, it occurred to the coach that had a 3-point line been available for Tina LeVigne, then his Warriors would probably have boarded the bus for the ride back to Wasilla at halftime.

He allowed himself no more than thirty minutes to review what had taken place, before quickly putting the tape away. The girls faced another challenge in Anchorage, in the semifinal game against Lathrop High from Fairbanks. The coach was worried.

After an emotional game like the one that occurred just hours earlier—certainly as nerve-racking and draining as any basketball game Teeguarden had ever seen—the prospect of a letdown loomed large. There was no possibility that the girls could duplicate their effort two nights in a row. Sure, his girls were driven, mature, and certainly not inclined to overconfidence. But they were still only human.

Also, Wasilla had beaten Lathrop in the regular season, something that would not work in their favor in a state tournament rematch. Just ask the East High Thunderbirds.

The Warriors would probably be primed and ready mentally, but the fiery and furious expenditure of physical resources from the opening round game, a full-force uphill climb from the opening tip to the final heart-stopping second, might take a toll. Lathrop's opening round win over Petersburg, on the other hand, had been a lopsided contest, and throughout most of the four quarters, Lathrop had, for the most part, been merely going through the motions. So the purple-and-gold Malamutes should be well rested. If ever there was a "trap" game, this one might be it.

Lathrop would be motivated, for sure. The Fairbanks school had an athletic heritage that extended well beyond

Wasilla's sporting past. The Malamutes rifle team was usually the best in the United States, and so was their cross-country ski team, but basketball, for years, had been a high-priority concern for the whole city. The Lathrop High School building had been constructed in 1954, but before that, Lathrop had been the original Fairbanks High, the team that had played Petersburg in the original all-Alaska state championship tourney in 1928.

Letter jackets awarded to Malamutes' athletes did not bear the letter "L" for Lathrop, but rather an "F" in honor of the old tradition held over from the days of Fairbanks High.

As he had done the day before, Teeguarden preceded his team to Anchorage so that he could watch the opening game on the semifinal marquis, which would match Service High against the other school from Fairbanks, Monroe Catholic. If anything, he was hoping that Service might win the game because of his apprehensions over what the Monroe Rams might offer the Warriors in a Saturday championship game.

To beat East, the task had been to slow down Tina LeVigne, because Teeguarden thought his lineup was superior to the four girls the T-Birds put on the court. Monroe's Rams had five lightning quick starters, and to concentrate on stopping one player would be a fatal tactic. On the overall standpoint of team play, Monroe did not take a back seat to Wasilla, and because of their team speed, the Rams provided the capacity to wear the Warriors down.

Service won the game and advanced to the finals, but that was a contest that left Teeguarden shaking his head. At no point in his coaching career would Teeguarden ever accuse a game official of costing a team of his a game. But he could do that in a game that did not involve him, and the aftermath of the Monroe–Service game left him with the strong impression that the Rams had lost because they had been home-cooked, jobbed, screwed—whatever verb might be applicable to a contest in which the zebras played a big role in an unfair outcome.

The highlight, or nadir, of the occasion happened in the fourth quarter, when the outcome was still in doubt. A player that Teeguarden recognized as "one of the Hadjukovich girls"—the Hadjukovich family being a Fairbanks legend that produced top players in all sports at Monroe Catholic for three generations—had been set up at the top of the key, standing dead still to face a Service fast game.

Hadjukovich got clobbered—pancaked was the way Teeguarden described the play to Assistant Coach Randall. To Teeguarden's amazement, the man with the whistle called a blocking foul on Hadjukovich, as she lay on the court flat on her back. It was the worst call the Wasilla coach had ever seen.

Well, better them than us, he thought.

Teeguarden was grateful for what he saw when the school bus arrived from Wasilla. The girls were wearing the same game face he'd seen the night before. The mood of the girls before the Lathrop game was one of quiet and grim determination. They were getting close and would not allow the big prize to slip away because of anything but total effort.

When the game started, the coach could tell right away that the kamikaze charge against East had indeed left some aftereffects. The keen edge had been dulled. His girls' shooting touch seemed to have abandoned them. Even more vexing was the condition of Sarah Heath. She had not appeared to have been significantly handicapped by her bum ankle in the T-Birds' fracas. Here against Fairbanks, Sarah was clearly favoring her sore leg. She dragged herself up and down the court as if an invisible hundred-pound weight had been chained to her left ankle.

Early in the second quarter, the score was tied at 15. Then, slowly at first, the Warriors' dead legs seemed to regain some of their spring. Wasilla began to pull away. The Warriors would never trail, or even be threatened by, Lathrop for the remainder of the contest. The lead was safe enough to Teeguarden to rest Sarah off and on over the course of the game.

When it was over, Wasilla had won it, 62–51, although the contest had not really been that close. The performance had been anything but a masterpiece, though. After the raw exhilaration from the night before, the mood of the team after the semifinal victory was by contrast one of overall relief.

The coach's evaluation of his team's Lathrop performance was "too many turnovers and low IQ fouls." The Warriors had done what had to be done, though, and the championship game was at hand.

Chapter 16

There are strange things done in the midnight sun
By the men who moil for gold
The arctic trails have their secret tales
That would make your blood run cold;
The Northern Lights have seen queer sights,
But the queerest they ever did see
Was that night on the marge of Lake Lebarge
I cremated Sam McGee

    —Poem by Robert Service, based on a true story

Most American high schools are named after either neighborhoods or dead presidents. So leave it to an Alaskan city to build a school and christen it in honor of a poet whose topics and themes glorified the activities of gamblers, thieves, drunks, barroom floozies, and opportunists of dubious distinction—in other words, the people who made Alaska great. His work was straightforward, and not drenched by the sappy symbolism that turns on supercilious academics but dulls the senses of readers endowed with sharper minds.

Robert Service was born in England, gravitated to the American northwest, and then into Canada. A wanderer and borderline bum with a natural knack for rhyming schemes, he would wind up in Dawson City during the latter years of the gold rush, working as a bank clerk. And with his talent for rhyming, he was also able to pick up tips in a saloon reciting poems like "Casey at the Bat" and "Gunga Din."

It was the saloonkeeper who recommended to Service that he might try to produce some original material. His patrons were getting bored. A bolt of inspiration struck Service, and he rushed to the bank late at night to pen "The Shooting of Dan McGrew," and was almost shot himself by a guard who mistook Service for a burglar.

Hats off to Anchorage for remembering Service, the people's poet, when a new school just off Abbott Road opened in 1971. The likes of Robert Frost, Emily Dickinson, and William Butler Yeats are held in higher esteem by literary elitists, but there aren't any high schools named after *them*.

He lived until 1958, and it's only too bad that Robert Service was not around to witness the events that took place in Anchorage in March 1982. Service might have written three or four snappy stanzas that he could have entitled "The Taming of Doreen Augeak." It would have been his best work.

The gymnasium at West High was a spacious facility, built to hold as many as seven thousand spectators for basketball events, and the facility was nearly filled to capacity for the finals of the Alaska girls basketball championships, the AAA division that contained the largest schools in the state.

The finalists were Service High against Wasilla High, the tank town Valley Trash and perpetual underdogs from the school with barely a high enough enrollment to qualify for AAA status. The occasion marked the third consecutive March that the Warriors had attained the finals, although they previously only saw their hopes shattered, first by Anchorage East in 1980, then Kodiak in 1981. The smart money leaned toward Wasilla scoring a championship loser's hat trick. Over the course of the long season, Wasilla had been beaten five times. They had lost to Anchorage East, Anchorage, Bartlett, Kodiak, and twice to Kenai. Service, on the other hand, had defeated the latter three with relative ease after whipping Kenai by 10 points in the tournament quarterfinals, and its coach had actually bemoaned what he identified as his absence of a "killer instinct," implying that his team should have won by 20 or more.

The Service Cougars, wearing green and gold, were performing in front of their hometown fans. The team's confidence was buttressed by two distinctive wins in that same West High gym over Kenai and Monroe Catholic from Fairbanks. The latter win had been accomplished via the aid and comfort of the game officials. It was not guaranteed that the Cougars' cause would receive that kind of reinforcement again, but it was certain that the whistle-bearing men wearing vertical black-and-white stripes would not go out of their way to do any favors for the visitors.

Bob Ferguson, the Service coach, was convinced that if his star gunner, Doreen Augeak, was on her game, and she almost always was, then the outcome was as good as sealed anyway. Augeak was a tallish guard, endowed with a perfectly proportioned basketball body. She was a native Aleut who had arrived on Ferguson's doorstep the previous summer. Augeak had traveled from her hometown in Barrow, the capital city of Middle of Nowhere, to attend a basketball camp in Anchorage.

The circumstances of why she chose to remain in the big city for her senior season had never been fully determined, but she had. Opposing teams never really came forward with any claims that Augeak was a ringer. Residential requirements for high school athletes in Alaska were lenient, given the migratory habits of the people in the state, and according to the letter of the law, Doreen Augeak was street-legal.

Throughout the season, Doreen had played like a girls basketball version of Pistol Pete Maravich. She was polished, a superior ball-handler capable of scoring in barrage-like bursts, 10 or 12 points in four or five minutes, that demoralized opponents and set them rocking back on their heels. Doreen was a Native American version of East's Tina LeVigne, and she spelled nothing but trouble for the Warriors.

All season, Coach Don Teeguarden had drawn up winning strategies to mitigate the skills of players like Augeak, and the team rehearsed those tactics in practice until they had the defensive scheme down pat. The coach of the Warriors, the man who had understood virtually nothing about the fine arts of girls basketball, had in a few years evolved into something of a perfectionist, and the 1981–1982 Warriors were a highly practice-oriented team.

But with the state tournament format calling for three games in three days, there had been no time for the practice and preparation that served as the blueprint for Wasilla's winning ways.

The championship contest had been scheduled as an afternoon affair, and the girls arrived at the school around 8 a.m. on a Saturday morning. Teeguarden did not want his team to arrive at West High School too early. The notion of killing time for a couple of hours might impair their pregame concentration. Still, he had to leave ample time for the forty-five-mile ride down to Anchorage, just on the off chance the bus broke down. Stranger things had been known to occur.

When the team rolled out for that final trek down from Wasilla to Anchorage, past the frozen Lake Lucille and across the Knik River, along the serpentine highway that wove through the snow-bedecked spires of the Chugach Mountains, they were accompanied by an escort of cars decorated in red. The whole town of Wasilla was bearing down on Anchorage, trashy and proud.

The AA championship game was underway when the Warriors arrived. A seeming eternity would elapse before the big show would mount center stage. Teeguarden was hoping that his team might stay laid back and focused, all at the same time, but how could they accomplish that? You couldn't have it both ways.

Finally, at last, it was time for the girls to trot onto the court for the pregame drills. The Wasilla side of the gym was already crammed, and the girls were greeted with loud cheers, and across the way, the backers of the home team were roaring as well.

Assistant Coach Cordell Randall watched intently as the Service girls warmed up. He marveled at Doreen Augeak, who was the portrait of serenity as she stood twenty feet from the basket, lobbing shot after shot. She never missed. Service posed a serious threat, for sure. Unlike the Warriors, with Heyde Kohring and Wanda Strutko, the Cougars did not have a player who stood six feet or taller. But three of the starters were five foot eleven, so on the whole, Service would take the court with more size than the Warriors.

Coach Teeguarden concentrated on his own team. He would need all five starters, plus Michelle Carney and Katie Port off the bench, to be at the absolute acme of their games if Wasilla hoped to prevail. Sarah Heath was his prime concern.

Teeguarden knew all too well that his point guard, who would be critical in the scheme to slow down Doreen Augeak, would be playing hurt. He knew that if anybody could perform on one-and-a-half legs, it was Sarah. She had honed her mental toughness during those grinding hours preparing for cross-country races and had mastered the mind-over-matter concept with an outlook that simply went, "If you don't mind it, it doesn't matter."

The coach could only hope for the best.

His team retreated to the locker room for one last pre-game mini-meeting. Teeguarden had not prepared any versions of a "win one for the Gipper" oratory. That had never been his style, and this was no time to come across like a phony.

He looked at his players, and in slow and measured tones declared, "Okay. You've got a great opportunity here. Let's take advantage of it." And that was all he said.

Back out on the court, it was time for the player introductions. The voice of the public address announcer boomed through the arena. "Starting at forward for the Service Cougars, a five-eleven senior, number twenty-eight, Shelly Kohinka!"

Kohinka trotted out to midcourt. Then, "Starting at forward for the Wasilla Warriors, a six-foot sophomore, number thirty-two, Wanda Strutko!"

Wanda advanced onto the court and shook hands with her counterpart, Kohinka. That ritual went on for starters on both teams. Doreen Augeak was the last of the Cougars to be announced. Augeak was a strikingly handsome young woman with thick raven-black hair, and she wore a black headband.

Finally, the tenth player was presented. "Starting at guard for Wasilla, a five-five senior and co-captain, number twenty-two, Sarah Heath!"

The girl who had worked like a field hand for three years, who one year earlier had literally begged her coaches for an opportunity to play, only to be demoted to the junior varsity team for additional seasoning, would at last experience the payoff for her labors. With the West High gym having been transformed into a braying bedlam of several thousand spectators, Sarah loped proudly onto the polished hardwood and pressed the flesh with Doreen Augeak. The girls returned to the bench, the starters pulled off their warm-up shirts, formed a circle with the Warriors mascot joining in, put their hands together, and in unison, yelled, "Let's go!" This would be their finest hour, and defeat was not an option.

At courtside, the Wasilla radio play-by-play boys, Hugh Mathison and Curt Menard, were giddy. "The Warriors fans are here in droves!" Mathison shouted. Indeed, the KABN ratings for the championship game would probably register a season low. The whole town of Wasilla was crammed into the Anchorage gym, so nobody would be listening to the game that Mathison and Menard were announcing.

Heyde Kohring, with her blonde hair pulled back into a ponytail, used every centimeter of her six-foot frame to win the jump ball that opened the game and tipped it to Jackie Conn. The Warriors set up their attack, but right away a whistle sounded. Karen Bush had been called with an offensive foul. The Wasilla fans reacted at once. "Boo! Boo!"

That was a non-shooting foul, and Service advanced quickly on the attack. Augeak dribbled the basketball across midcourt, stopped at the key, looked inside, and then, without hesitation, launched a twenty-foot salvo. *Swish*. First blood. The Cougars fans lunged to their feet. No, an earth-quake had not occurred, but inside the gym, the structure seemed to tremble.

The Warriors staged a counterattack. Karen Bush advanced the ball down the court and whipped the ball to Sarah Heath on the left wing. Sarah fired a blistering pass to Strutko, who turned, put the ball off the glass, and scored. The game was 2–2, and the battle was on.

Augeak came back, and without even considering passing the ball, launched another set shot. This time, the ball didn't go in, but the pattern was set. Doreen was making it all too clear that she intended to carry the Service team on her shoulders alone. Playing there in the championship game, in what Las Vegas stars call the Big Room, Augeak was primed to deliver a command performance.

The first quarter was tight and was played at the white-hot tempo of the East game. Both teams committed four turnovers in the opening minutes, and players on both sides pressed the issue, playing with an attitude of wild-eyed desperation, trying to overachieve. The pressure that went with a state championship game was affecting the quality of play. The only player on the side of the Warriors maintaining any sense of control was Strutko, the sophomore. Dominant underneath, she banked in three baskets with Cougars draped all over her. She would score 9 of Wasilla's first 11 points. The other four players were off target, and Strutko alone was keeping the Warriors in the game.

The radio guys from Wasilla were at top form. "Here's a substitution for Service. Number thirty-three," said Curt Menard. "There's not a number thirty-three on the roster. We'll just call her the Dark Horse." Moments later, he would describe a play with, "The Cougars try to work the ball inside to Kohinka . . . and . . . the Dark Horse throws it away!"

From the standpoint of Robert Service High, this was not the kind of beginning they had wanted or anticipated. During every previous game of the season, the Cougars owned the lead, and usually by a lot after the opening quarter. Their coach knew that in the championship game, his girls, and most especially, Doreen Augeak, were nervous, and he did not know what to do about it. As the game entered the second quarter, Wasilla led 11–10, but neither team was anywhere close to establishing an element of momentum.

If the players were being thrown off balance by the intensity of what was at stake, it was just as bad for the fans. A Warriors fan, sitting near courtside, yelled at the referee in a voice that could have been heard all the way back to Wasilla. "THREE SECONDS, YOU IDIOT!" Five seconds later, he was at it again. "HEY REF! HOW ABOUT

CALLING A THREE SECOND VIOLATION EVERY NOW AND THEN, EVEN IF THIS IS IN ANCHORAGE!"

If the officials heard him, they did not seem to pay attention.

But the Warriors were slowly beginning to take charge. Doreen Augeak was firing at will, and suddenly, shooting blanks. It was as if a transparent lid was covering the basket. With Wasilla suddenly ahead, 17–12, Augeak was charged with a foul as she collided with Kohring while going after a rebound. She whipped off her headband in a gesture of disgust and ran her fingers through her hair. Things were not going as Augeak had planned. On every possession, the Warriors put a different defender in her face. Heath. Then Bush. Then Conn. The triumvirate that had slowed down Tina LeVigne was doing the same to Doreen Augeak. From Don Teeguarden's perspective, he could hardly have asked for more.

The Cougars were beginning to look more than vulnerable. Michelle Carney had been sent in to replace Strutko, who picked up her third foul. Carney, as she had all season, provided an instant spark and fired in a shot from the corner.

Jackie Conn stole the ball from Service's Ruth Brodie and led a fast break the other way. She fed a great pass to Kohring, who was in full stride, and put in the layup. That was the play of the game, until then, and Wasilla pulled ahead 21–10. The lead would reach 13 points, and the Cougars would claw their way back. Doreen Augeak might have been frigid from the field, but she was deadly at the foul line. And while Augeak had been beyond erratic, heaving up one brick after another from every spot on the court, Coach Ferguson, situated on the bench, appeared to wince every time any other Cougar player took a shot.

Teeguarden knew that he was watching a winnable situation, but the hay was not in the barn yet. Not by a long shot. Service narrowed the lead to 7 points at halftime, and Sarah Heath was limping. He knew for sure that when, or if, Augeak regained her shooting touch, this contest would get dicey in a hurry.

Teeguarden didn't tell his team much of anything at halftime. He was not about to suggest any real adjustments. The girls had taken complete charge during that surge in the middle of the second quarter. Of the listings on the basketball coach's Ten Commandments, item number one dictated: "Thou shalt not try to fix what ain't broken."

The girls were hungry, he could tell, and the championship was only two eight-minute quarters away; so close that the kids could practically taste it.

After halftime, it became clear that the Warriors would not choke. They scored the first two baskets of the third quarter, and Augeak, still attempting to put on a heroic one-woman show, fired from thirty feet and missed by a mile. After Wasilla was called for traveling, the fan who had been berating the refs yelled, "GIVE THE BALL TO AUGEAK. SHE'S THE BEST PLAYER WASILLA HAS!"

The ball did, in fact, go to Augeak, but before she could shoot yet again, Karen Bush, sneaked behind her, and quick as a cobra, snatched the ball, ran like the quarter-miler that she had been, sped down the court, and, while all of the girls on the Wasilla bench leaped to their feet and waved towels, put in a layup, drew a foul, and completed the 3-point play. The Warriors were once again up by 13. Twice more, Karen Bush would duplicate that play, stealing the ball from Augeak and driving all alone to the basket to drop in an uncontested layup. Those three outstanding plays would account for all 7 points that Bush scored in the championship game. But more important than the impact the points had made on the scoreboard had been the emotional element. Those three steals against a team trying to fight and punch its way back into the game had resulted in morale-shattering knockout shots.

Augeak was not about to quit. But she missed again, and on the radio, Curt Menard said, "Maybe Doreen ought to change her name to Remington, or Smith and Wesson, or something like that. She's shooting holes in this place!" Then she tried to steal the ball from Sarah Heath and was charged with her third foul. She acknowledged the call with an angry gesture that looked like she was throwing a rock at the scorer's table.

As the seconds ticked down the third quarter, the Warriors who had been sloppy and hurried in the earlier portions of the game were beginning to function with precision. Jackie Conn took the basketball to the side of the court and stood still dribbling the ball while she sized up the scene. Then, quickly, Conn whipped the ball to Heath in the corner, who fired a stunningly quick pass to Kohring, who, graceful as a swan, turned and banked in a lovely reverse layup. *Zip. Zap.* That was a terrific play—Red Auerbach's Boston Celtics never did any better, and all of a sudden, the Warriors were ahead by 15 points.

The Cougars, playing with equal measures of heart and guts, cut that lead to 11 at the end of the period when Augeak connected from outside at the buzzer. But after three quarters, she was three of fourteen from the field. On the Cougars' bench, Coach Bob Ferguson looked as though he might throw up.

Whatever he told his team seemed to work. The Cougars mounted a full-court press on defense, stayed patient on offense, and when Augeak came up with a steal, she made a great pass to Ruth Brody, who dribbled twice and scored from fifteen feet, and for the first time since the half, Wasilla's lead slipped to single digits.

The Robert Service Cougars were not able to establish a genuine momentum swing. Still, the Anchorage team was like a lingering summer cold that would never really go away. Also, Strutko was playing, but saddled with four fouls, and Heath picked up her fourth as well on a play in which Sarah went down on the floor hard. Her ankle felt like it was on fire.

Teeguarden took her out of the game, replacing Heath with Katie Port.

Service continued to apply the press, but it was Jackie Conn, the girl endowed with a natural sense of court smarts, the girl who *just gets it,* who stepped forward to crack the code. On consecutive possessions, she first employed a classic pump fake of a shot from the baseline, and converted both ends of a one-and-one and then, after a Service turnover, Conn inbounded the ball with a three-quarter court pass to a wide open Kohring, who scored the easy layup. The Warriors would lead by ten, 49–39, with five minutes left on the clock. That was the same scoreboard clock that Don Teeguarden was tempted to attack with a hammer. To him, time was literally standing still. The seconds seemed to limp along in slow motion. Was this thing ever going to end? His nerves felt tight as piano wire.

Two sudden turnovers, and two baskets by the Cougars, one by Ruth Brodie, the other by Stacy Russell, and with slightly under four minutes, Robert Service sliced the margin to six, 51–46, and they had the ball again. Naturally, the Cougars tried to pass the ball to Doreen Augeak, a move that Jackie Conn fully anticipated. Conn made some contact in the process of intercepting the pass, and Augeak collapsed on the court.

Hugh Mathison screamed into his microphone. "Augeak is down!" The girl that her coach had described as being the most valuable player in all of Alaska was twisting in agony. "What's wrong with her, Hugh?" Curt asked on the air.

"Don't know," answered Mathison. "Looks like she's got something in her eye."

What happened was that Doreen Augeak had gotten the wind knocked out of her. She stayed down for a full two minutes, surrounded by coaches, two trainers, and four teammates. Finally, the trainers pulled her to her feet and assisted the star off the court. The entire Wasilla cheering section stood up and gave the girl a loud, echoing ovation. The shots had not fallen for Augeak on that championship Saturday, but her incessant drive on both ends of the court had provided the fans with an exhibition for the ages.

But she would not return to the game. Her tank was empty. She was spent, beaten down, and shattered, and probably wishing that she had never left her home up in Barrow on the banks of the Arctic Ocean. In the game account that appeared in the Sunday edition of the *Anchorage Daily News,* it was reported that "when Augeak left the game exhausted, so were the Cougars' chances of overtaking Wasilla."

Certainly, most of the people in the West High gym were thinking the same thing, but that was not quite the case. The Cougars would not fold. During the final frenetic three minutes, they fought like Marines trying to plant the flag on Iwo Jima. They took on a "let's win this one for Doreen" spirit. Every rebound was landing in Service's hands. As the seconds crept by, ever so slowly, Service came back to narrow the Wasilla lead to 4 points. With fewer than thirty seconds to play, the Cougars got the ball back. Teeguarden called time, and put Sarah Heath back onto the court.

The game and the state championship were on the line now, and, crippled or not, the Warriors needed their most reliable defensive player in the game.

With twenty-three seconds left, Service's Ruth Brodie drew a foul. She would step to the line with a 1-and-1 opportunity that could cut what had once been a 15-point Wasilla lead to 2, and if that happened, the Cougars had enough time to make a steal and another quick basket to complete an impossible comeback.

"Well . . . uh . . . it comes down to this, fans," said dentist-turned-broadcaster Curt Menard. He sounded like he was having a stroke.

Ruth Brodie, very soon, toed the line, bounced the basketball five times, took a deep breath, bent her knees, and shot. The ball rolled around the rim, and then out, and ten players lunged from the rebound in a violent ballet of flying bodies. The officials, had they wanted to, could have called a foul on every player on the floor during the crazy melee.

First, Strutko seemed to have the ball, then Kohinka stole it from Wanda, and then, in intense hand-to-hand combat, Sarah Heath yanked the ball away from Kohinka. Brodie grabbed Heath from behind, almost pulling Sarah to the floor.

Tweet! The foul was on Brodie. Ten seconds remained in the high school basketball careers of the Wasilla seniors—Heath, Conn, and Kohring—and Sarah, who had not scored a point in the entire game, would have a free throw opportunity that, if she made it, would ice the game and complete the dream.

She looked over her shoulder at the scoreboard and clock, as if to confirm what might be about to happen. Jackie Conn walked over and patted Sarah on the back. Chuck Heath had left his seat in the stands and walked to the baseline with his camera. He wanted to capture this moment. From her position on the court, Conn spotted Chuck. She smiled and winked.

Unlike Ruth Brodie moments earlier, Sarah did not bounce the ball or draw the deep breath. Without a second's hesitation, she put the ball up. It hit the front of the rim, bounced onto the backboard and back down through the net. Wasilla was up by five, 58–53, and they were safe. Everybody who attended the girls championship game in Anchorage that day would recall that when Sarah Heath scored the one and only point that would be listed next to her name in the championship box score, it seemed as if all the air had been sucked from the building. The high anxiety was finally, at long last, over.

"And the Wasilla Warriors are the 1982 Alaska girls basketball state champions!" Hugh Mathison screamed. "What a great day for Don Teeguarden! For the last two years, he was the bridesmaid. And now, he's the . . . bride!"

The announcer was beside himself, along with the Warriors fans, coaches, and players on the bench. If Sarah Heath were feeling the same hysterical exuberance, she certainly didn't display it. After the shot fell, she had shown no reaction whatsoever.

Her second shot missed, and both Teeguarden and Cordell Randall ran down the sideline, frantically waving their arms, imploring the girls not to guard anybody or draw a foul. A half-court heave by Kohinka that would have altered the final score, but not the outcome of the state championship game, thudded against the wall behind the baseline, and the sound of the buzzer triggered a stampede of Wasilla fans onto the court for a war dance of ecstatic delirium. March Madness indeed.

During the postgame awards ceremony that happened at a velvet-draped dais at center court, Sarah Heath was the first player summoned to receive her state championship medallion. She looked at it like it was the Hope Diamond.

The radio combo, the fellows from KABN "The Cabin," cornered Teeguarden to seek his reaction of the events. As usual, he was the living portrait of understatement. "You're at the top of the coaching world, Don," Curt Menard raved. "Well, this is a group of girls who really make you look good," Teeguarden said. "I don't know what parents do to make kids like these. But whatever it is, I want to do it with my own."

On the other side of the court, Bob Ferguson, the Service coach, seemed almost too crestfallen to talk. "I was really convinced that this would be our year. But after two playoff wins, we had a physical letdown today," he told the *Anchorage Daily News.* "We were too high, and they were so nervous, they took themselves out of the game.

"They got it back together, finally. But it was too late."
Two years later, Ferguson would finally realize the sensation of winning the state championship. But that still would never compensate for the pain that he was feeling as the sun set on Service's basketball season. Teeguarden, who had suffered the same experience himself, would have been the first to sympathize. Truly, he felt bad for his coaching opponent.

According to Don Teeguarden's recollection, the postgame setting in the locker room of the Warriors was one of shouts, hugs, and tears of joy. In the end, the championship victory had been the product of each of the players offering whatever individual asset she offered to the team: Wanda Strutko, using her God-given physical strength to dominate the play underneath the basket; Heyde Kohring, putting her height and almost delicate scoring and rebounding touch to maximum use; Jackie Conn, the flawless-as-usual decision-maker coming up with huge plays when it had mattered the most; Karen Bush, the defensive stalwart, with her spectacular baskets that had resulted from key steals; and Sarah Heath, playing in pain, stacking up assist after assist, and all the while pestering Doreen Augeak until the Service superstar had been completely neutralized. That team had been a finely tuned engine that would have burned up against Service had any one of the five moving parts not been functioning smoothly the whole game.

Before returning to Wasilla, Teeguarden decided that his girls should celebrate in style. He directed the bus driver to stop at an Anchorage pizza parlor. Inside the girls ate, while the state championship trophy sat on display atop a table next to the salad bar. As for the coach, he would remember never enjoying a meal more than this one.

Epilogue

I n a memorable snippet of dialogue from Ernest Hemingway's *The Sun Also Rises*, a member of what might have been known as Britain's impoverished aristocracy Jake Barnes and Lady Brett Ashley et al. met for a drunken holiday in Spain.

Somebody asks the old Brit an awkward question: "How did you manage to blow your vast fortune?"

"Two ways," he said. "Gradually at first, and then all of a sudden."

That aptly describes the course of change in American life that has occurred since 1982, when the Wasilla girls won the Alaskan state basketball championship and in the process altered the identity and self-concept of the community that was their hometown.

To look back on and examine the year of the Warriors' title—1982—that becomes a study in the vanishing age of innocence. In those early years of the Ronald Reagan presidency, day-to-day existence was more simple and much more affordable. People could buy a top-quality new car for seven grand. Jobs were abundant. The term "outsourcing" did not exist. People employed by American companies in the technology field did not live somewhere other than the United States. American industry actually manufactured products. Nobody had heard of AIDS or global warming.

The American middle class, the backbone of the society, was thriving. Air travel was not an ordeal tantamount to the extraction of wisdom teeth. Terrorist attacks were things that happened overseas, and not very often. No space shuttles had blown up. O. J. Simpson was a name associated with football. In the realm of sports journalism, the top stories concentrated on what the athlete did in the game, and not what he or she had to say about it afterward.

The USA was a better place in 1982 than it is now. Not only were the movies better, but most of the best-selling songs did not sound like the derailment of a commuter train.

People living in Wasilla in 1982 would hardly recognize their town now. It is the sixth largest city in Alaska, and a referendum to move the state capital from Juneau to Wasilla was defeated, but not by much.

There is, however, one aspect of the landscape from 1982 that has not changed: the people who played on the

Wasilla team that shocked the state with their unprecedented championship run.

In 2007, the Alaska School Activities Association invited the whole team and the coaches for a reunion in Anchorage to commemorate the twenty-fifth anniversary of their triumph. The reunion was scheduled on a Saturday to coincide with the state championship game and the culmination of March Madness. Fittingly, the Wasilla Warriors would be one of the participants.

That 1982 team prevailed on the basis of high character athletes, living a life based on family and faith. So while the girls have gone their separate ways, their lives adhere to the identical standard of values that was there before.

Almost all of the girls from the 1982 team attended the event, a catered reception, inside the arena where the championship games would take place. Some brought their children, and a few grandkids were there, too. People brought scrapbooks and mementos from the day they would never forget, and copies of the Mat-Su Valley *Frontiersman* that declared **CINDERELLA TEAM WINS STATE**. In Alaska, Cinderella would need to wear fur-lined boots, because glass slippers won't hack it there in the wintertime. But the description was appropriate.

Don Teeguarden, who had moved to Washington state and was still coaching at a high school near Spokane, was there, reexperiencing the only state championship he would win in his coaching career. Other than the fact that his mustache had taken on a silver hue, he looked exactly the same. He was overwhelmed at being reunited with his kids, after a quarter of century, and while exchanging hugs Teeguarden, on a couple of occasions, blinked back some tears.

The same could be said for Cordell Randall, who had gained perhaps five pounds, but unless he tinted his hair, had seemingly not aged a day. By 2007, Cordell was teaching second grade in Merced, California.

Randall stood before the old team and said, "You girls gave me memories of a lifetime. One of the highlights of my life was to have the opportunity to coach you and be a part of that championship season."

Everybody applauded.

Sarah Heath Palin, at that time the governor of Alaska, went into the locker room of the Warriors and read a card she'd prepared for the girls of 2007, wishing them well in the championship game that was about to come up. The girls giggled and cheered. They would not let the governor down. On the occasion of the reunion, Wasilla beat the Juneau Crimson Bears, 51–48, the first state title won by the Wasilla girls since the 1982 event. In 2007, the boys won it, too, a first for Wasilla. The front page of the Sunday *Frontiersman* proclaimed **VALLEY OF CHAMPIONS!**

Perhaps it was serendipity, but the presence of Teeguarden's girls of winter and the aura of their legacy had played a part in a great day for basketball in Wasilla.

After the event, the girls parted once more, and that reunion might have marked the last time they would ever be together as a group again.

Where are they now?

Karen Bush is a homemaker living in Colorado. Her little sister Kim, who was a backup on the 1982 team, works for the school system in Fairbanks.

Katie Port is a private investigator in Minot, North Dakota.

Michelle Carney, who had become a psychologist, has her own consulting business in Glendale, Arizona.

Wanda Strutko is an emergency room nurse in Wasilla.

Heyde Kohring, who went on to play college basketball at Murray State, still lives in Kentucky and teaches children with special needs.

Jackie Conn is a detective on the police force in Anchorage.

Among some of the other personalities who appeared in this book, Paul Riley, the pastor at the Wasilla Assembly of God, is retired, but still lives in Wasilla and attends the services.

Jerry Yates, the coach at Wasilla Junior High who showed the girls the pathway to the championship, is retired and lives in Palmer.

Roger Nelles, the boys basketball coach at Wasilla in 1982, is retired and still lives there.

Chuck and Sally Heath are alive and very well in Wasilla, along with their forty-year-old Maytag washing machine. Chuck ran his Boston Marathon in 1982. He finished in under four hours, but the heat got to him and he walked the last two miles. After training for the event during the winter months along the Palmer-Wasilla Highway, the early-May clime in Boston made him feel like he was running in the jungles of Borneo.

Todd Palin, a key player on the 1982 Wasilla boys team that nearly won state, is a professional snow mobile driver and three-time winner of the Iron Horse competition that passes along the same trails as the Iditarod dogsled race.

Sarah Heath Palin is involved in politically related activities. The ankle that she injured in the regional tournament in 1982 still bothers her to this day.

Acknowledgments

I've now written seven-and-a-half books over the course of the last sixteen years, and have never relied on the assistance and goodwill of others more than in this one.

Not even close. So I am going to extend my heartfelt thanks to the following folks.

First, there is Cheryl Chapman, the former book editor at *The Dallas Morning News* who relocated in Anchorage about five years ago. She chose Anchorage over another job opportunity in Kabul, Afghanistan, on the basis of something her mother told her: "It is always a good idea to try to live somewhere where you look like everybody else." Cheryl offered background and insight that were crucial to the proposal that led to the publication of this book. She occasionally sends e-mails with stories from the *Anchorage Daily News,* where she is the garden editor, that tell the real story of Alaska—stories with headlines like: **BAREFOOT OCTOGENARIAN FELLS MOOSE**. Cheryl also supplied me with a copy of *Real Alaska* magazine, a slick and very amusing satire publication that is unique to anything in the United States.

Julia O'Malley is a writer at the *Anchorage Daily News* who produces what is, in my estimation, the best local column in the United States, and with the possible exception of Mike Royko, the best ever. Nobody captures the spirit of their community better than Julia does, and she really set me straight on the chapter in this book that is devoted to Alaskan women. Additionally, I wish to single out a man in Wasilla, Forrest Dow, who explained in very vivid terms what it is like to be an Alaskan.

Two individuals at Wasilla High School were immensely helpful. The current coach of the Warriors, Jeannie Truax-Hebert, provided a font of details about the ways and means of girls basketball in the state of Alaska. Her team won the state championship in 2011, and she thinks next season's team, which will fly all the way up to Barrow for its season opener, might very well win it again. I hope they do.

Assistant Principal Dan Michael, a former football player for the North Dakota State Fighting Sioux and who looks the part, took plenty of time out of a very busy day to provide me with info and a tour of the Wasilla High athletic facilities. It was Dan Michael who referred me to Gary Matthews, who is in charge of the Alaska School Activities Association in Anchorage. Gary offered some compelling facts and stories about the amazing saga of high school sports, past and present, in Alaska.

Gil Truitt lives in Sitka, Alaska, and is the world's leading authority on the history of high school basketball in Alaska, and particularly in the southeast part of the state. Gil has compiled a history book about the old days called *Past Days of Glory,* and his range of information on the topic is encyclopedic. He is the source of my favorite anecdote in this book in which the boys of the Sheldon Jackson boarding school got seasick on their trip to play Petersburg and vomited into their equipment bags.

Four coaches from Wasilla in 1982 were extraordinarily generous with their time and their memories. They are Don Teeguarden, Cordell Randall, Roger Nelles, and Jerry Yates. To talk to these men is to understand how the girls of Wasilla became a group that transcended the concept of "team."

Joe Vallely, my literary agent, the head of Flaming Star Literary Enterprises who lives in Virginia, was a crucial figure in the publication of this. What Joe does is actually offer encouragement to authors as these projects unfold, which is a rare thing these days among the people in his profession. Joe represented me previously when I wrote *Seasons in Hell,* and he has a keen eye for book topics that meander from the mainstream. He hangs in there when other agents wimp out.

Matt Martz, my editor at St. Martin's, and his publishing team are terrific. Matt's patience with the progress of this manuscript is unprecedented.

On the home front, the ceaseless support, advice, and assistance of my spouse of twenty-five years, Karen Greer Shropshire, has once again been absolutely invaluable.

And finally, I want to express my appreciation to my son Patrick who unselfishly provided me the use of his laptop after that piece-of-junk computer that was purchased at Best Buy blew up during the early stages of this project.

Mike Shropshire
Dallas, Texas
June 2011